A BOOK FOR ALL SEASONS

1950: We laughed until we wept with Sid Caesar, Imogene Coca and the rest of the Shows of Shows crew . . .

1956: TV newscasting changed forever with the appearance of a pair of casual, quip-trading reporters named Chet Huntley and David Brinkley . . .

1963: Haute cuisine became a national pastime when Julia Child wielded her chef's knife on TV . . .

1969: The first men landed on the moon and we saw it all on the tube . . .

Here it is, season-by-season, show-by-show, the excitement, the drama, the nostalgia of . . .

THE TELEVISION YEARS

THE TELEVISION YEARS

by Arthur Shulman and Roger Youman

POPULAR LIBRARY • NEW YORK

For Lily Ann and Joan

ACKNOWLEDGMENTS

We would like to express our gratitude to a number of organizations and persons who provided invaluable assistance in the preparation of this book. Our thanks to TV Guide magazine, ABC-TV, CBS-TV, NBC-TV, PBS, the Herbert Floyd Kasselle Estate, the International Communications Archives, and these individuals: Domenick Giofre, Vic Ghidalia, Shirley Imo, George Miller, Donald C. W. Mooney, Ken Regan and Mari Yanofsky.

INTRODUCTION

The Television Years. For some of us—the youngest among us—there never have been anything *but* television years. As these introductory paragraphs are written, in the fall of 1972, nearly half of the people living in the United States are less than 25 years old, which means that television has been a part of their lives since the day they were born. Tell them about the good old days before television and you might as well be describing the time of the Peloponnesian War.

The rest of us, however—including the authors of this book—were here before television was. We witnessed the arrival of this miraculous gadget. It seemed childlike and innocent, eager for our attention and affection. We played with it, laughed at it, marveled as it learned new tricks, and watched expectantly to see what it would do next. We have seen it grow into a powerful giant. Confident that it has us in its thrall, it is too big and strong to wonder whether we still love it, yet always worried that we may not respect it.

We can remember that first ugly set with the small screen and the fuzzy picture. Our memories of what we saw on that screen are fuzzy too. But we do remember. Our reactions to those early programs, and the ones that followed, have run the gamut from rapture to contempt, with a good deal of apathy in between. Still, we remember them. Some of them we look back upon fondly; others we would rather forget.

This book is designed to summon up those memories, in sharp focus, year by year, from the earliest days of television broadcasting to the present.

Television is primarily a visual experience. It is something you *watch*. There is nothing we can say in words about television that will recall its past as vividly as pictures will. And so, in this book, we will let the pictures speak for themselves, although we will observe television's custom and pause now and then for a brief message—a few words between pictures, to put things into historical perspective.

And away we go. . . .

THE YEARS OF THE PIONEERS

When was television born? You can pick any of several dates, depending on which of the earliest pioneers you choose to honor. But there is some validity in saying that it started in 1925, when John Logie Baird and Charles Francis Jenkins, working independently of each other on two sides of the Atlantic, both produced weak and blurry images on a screen. . . . Or in 1928, when WGY, Schenectady, went on the air three days a week. After that, progress is swift. . . . 1930: NBC opens an experimental TV transmitter in New York. . . . 1931: WICR goes on the air in New York, operated by Gimbel Bros. . . . 1932: CBS-TV reports on the Presidential election, to an estimated 7500 sets. . . . 1937: Seventeen experimental stations are operating. . . . 1938: NBC telecasts "Susan and God," with Gertrude Lawrence. . . . 1939: Allen B. DuMont puts the first all-electronic sets on the market. The opening of the New York World's Fair is televised. A Princeton–Columbia baseball game is the first TV sportscast. . . . 1940: "Pagliacci" is telecast from the Met. The Republican Convention is shown live. CBS airs the first colorcast. . . .

World's Fair: As President Franklin D. Roosevelt (A) opens the New York World's Fair in 1939, an NBC camera (B) telecasts the event to the handful of people who have TV sets.

1941: Commercial telecasting begins July 1. WNBT takes to the air with a Dodgers–Pirates game from Ebbets Field. The first commercial is the face of a Bulova clock, as an announcer intones the time (the commercial costs Bulova $9). Other programs that first day: A Lowell Thomas newscast, a USO show, *Uncle Jim's Question Bee* and a simulcast (radio and TV) of *Truth or Consequences*. . . . 1942: There are 10 stations on the air, but the war darkens them for the duration. . . . 1945: VE Day celebrations are telecast. So is the first commercial intercity event—the Army–Navy Game, from Philadelphia to New York. . . . 1947: Some 14,000 homes have sets now, and television creates its first regular programs —*Juvenile Jury*, *Kraft Television Theatre*, *Leave It to the Girls*, *Kukla, Fran and Ollie*, *Meet the Press*, *Howdy Doody* —and the first soap opera, *A Woman to Remember* (who is quickly forgotten). In 1947 viewers also see the opening of the 80th Congress, President Truman's State of the Union Address and, later that year, a visit to Truman in the White House. The World Series (Yankees vs. Dodgers) is watched for the first time by set owners in New York, Philadelphia, Washington, D.C., and Schenectady. . . . And so The Television Years begin.

THE YEARS OF THE PIONEERS

Howdy Doody: It's TV's first popular children's show, consisting of Buffalo Bob Smith, his freckle-faced puppet Howdy Doody, a clown called Clarabell, a changing cast of supporting characters and a "peanut gallery" filled with Howdy's loyal young fans. The intensity of their loyalty will be demonstrated anew in the 1970's, when Buffalo Bob becomes a hit again—on college campuses populated by the kids who sang along with him in the 1950's.

Kukla, Fran and Ollie: They start on Chicago television in 1947, go national in 1949 and will still be delighting children—and adults—in the 1970's. Burr Tillstrom is the gifted puppeteer and Fran Allison the human member of the Kuklapolitan Players.

Juvenile Jury: Jack Barry is the host of this early panel show in which "sage youngsters advise their contemporaries on perplexing personal problems." The jurors (l.-r.) are Michelle Fogel, Douglas Stewart and Joe Ward.

THE YEARS OF THE PIONEERS

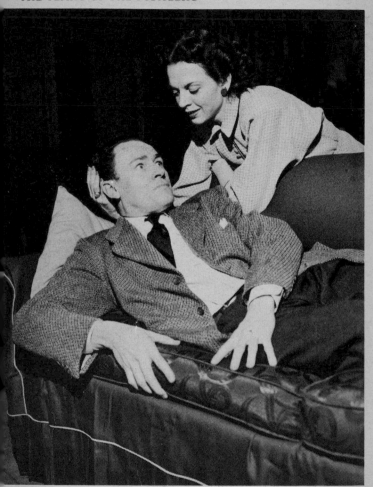

Kraft Television Theatre: Television's first—and most dura-ble—hour-long drama series begins May 7, 1947. In its first year it presents two plays a week on ABC and NBC—live, of course. One of them is "On Stage," starring E.G. Marshall and Barbara Joyce.

Kyle MacDonnell: The blonde singer becomes the first "sweetheart" of television viewers. Here, she poses with an airline pilot, Capt. Tom Gibbons.

THE YEARS OF THE PIONEERS

Roller Derby: Television brings this obscure sport a large, incredulous audience. Early viewers enjoy the violence, even if they aren't sure what the point of it all is. Here, Tuffy Brasuhn decks Terry Marie.

Bert Parks: He begins his TV career in 1947 with *Break the Bank* and goes on to become the medium's archetypal master of ceremonies, smiling his way through dozens of other game shows and, every September, the Miss America Pageant.

Douglas Edwards: His nightly newscasts begin during the 1947-48 season. He will be CBS News's anchor man until Walker Cronkite replaces him in 1963.

Paul Winchell: One of the first entertainers to have his own show is a ventriloquist. He arrives in 1947 with his dummies, Jerry Mahoney (left) and Knucklehead Smith.

THE YEARS OF THE PIONEERS

Leave It to the Girls: This panel series gives women their first opportunity to prove they're smarter than men. It begins in 1947 (although this publicity photo, shot later, shows— l.-r.—panelists Eloise McElhone and Vanessa Brown, producer Martha Rountree and "Father Time" uneasily welcoming the New Year of 1954).

Gene Autry: He rides into television from the movies and radio, astride his horse (Champion) and accompanied by his trusty sidekick (Pat Buttram). He'll stay in the TV saddle until a posse of "adult" Westerns overtakes him in the 1950's.

17

1948
THE YEAR OF UNCLE MILTIE

Enter Milton Berle. He wears outrageous costumes and he interrupts other performers, but he tickles the national funny-bone and his presence soon dominates the young medium. He is known as Mr. Television, and because of him there is a boom in TV set sales (at year's end they will total an estimated 190,000). . . . There are other notable variety entries this year: columnist Ed Sullivan begins the finger-pointing and grimaces that will trademark *Toast of the Town* (later *The Ed Sullivan Show*) for 23 years; a radio disc jockey, Arthur Godfrey, introduces show-biz tyros on *Talent Scouts;* and Ted Mack brings on *The Original Amateur Hour*. . . . Allen Funt's *Candid Microphone* (later it will be titled *Candid Camera*) is a 1948 starter. . . . Music fanciers have a wide selection: *The Voice of Firestone* debuts, TV's first full-length opera ("Otello") originates at the Met, and Eugene Ormandy conducts the Philadelphia Orchestra in the medium's first symphonic telecast. West Coast viewers see a mystery singer called *The Masked Spooner* (in the first Emmy awards, the Spooner will lose out to a puppet named *Judy Splinters*). . . . Quiz shows abound. There are *Who Said That?* (Bob Trout), *Winner Take All* (Bud Collyer), *Charade Quiz* (Bill Slater) and *Break the Bank* (Bert Parks). . . . Kids watch *Lucky Pup* and Ireene Wicker as *The Singing Lady;* their parents sometimes join them, as *The Lone Ranger* and *Hopalong Cassidy* ride into view. . . . *The Gloria Swanson Hour*, an interview show, bows in New York, while Jack Eigen conducts a talk marathon from the Copacabana night club. . . . House-wives can see *The Laytons*, an early soap opera; *Mary Kay and Johnny*, John Reed King's *The Missus Goes A'Shopping* and *The Wendy Barrie Show*. . . . Two dramatic giants debut: *Philco Playhouse* opens with "Dinner at Eight" (Peggy Wood, Dennis King) and *Studio One* offers "The Storm" (Margaret Sullavan). José Ferrer appears as Cyrano on *Philco*, a role he will repeat in later years. . . . John Cameron Swayze anchors *The Camel News Caravan*, and Don Hollenbeck teams with Edward R. Murrow on a CBS news show. . . . The Rose Bowl is televised for the first time (Michigan over USC, 49–0). . . . We learn about LS/MFT, and we are urged to "Use Ajax . . . bum bum . . . the foaming cleanser . . . bum bum bum bum bum."

Texaco Star Theater: Milton Berle (shown here with guest Gracie Fields) reigns as undisputed King of early television. Once, referring to Bishop Sheen, his competition on another network, Berle cracks: "We both work for the same boss— Sky Chief."

19

Ed Sullivan: They make jokes about his mangled syntax and herky-jerky movements, but Sullivan is a master showman with an unerring instinct about popular tastes. He presents the great (like Oscar Hammerstein II, playing piano here) and the not-so-great in a colorful parade of vaudeville and variety acts.

The Original Amateur Hour: Ted Mack (right, with announcer Dennis James) replaces the fabled Major Bowes in the TV version of this monument to nonprofessionalism. For more than two decades, Mack will patiently introduce washboard-strummers, baton flingers, and sopranos who come very close to hitting the right notes.

21

The Lone Ranger: Clayton Moore is the masked man, and Tonto is played by Jay Silverheels. ''Hi-yo, Silver . . . Away'' and ''Kemo Sabay'' are the oft-repeated bywords of the show.

Hopalong Cassidy: William Boyd is Hoppy, and he repeats his screen success with a new generation of television children.

1948

Philco Playhouse: A young producer named Fred Coe gives this show its creative impetus. Though it leans toward original scripts and new faces, *Philco* also does adaptations like "Rebecca" (shown here). In this cast are (l.-r.) Bob Stanton, Mary Anderson, Florence Reed, Bert Lytell and Bramwell Fletcher.

Studio One: Worthington Miner is the producer and driving force behind this acclaimed dramatic series. In the play shown here, Mercedes McCambridge stars in "Kyra Zelas."

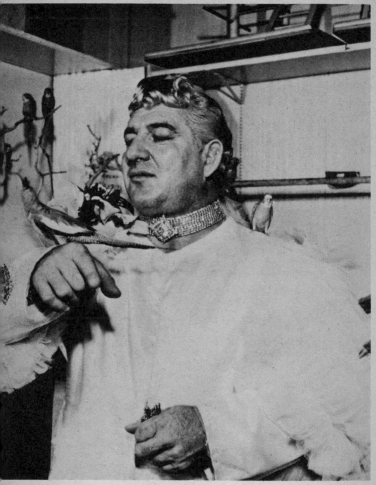

Wrestling: The grunt-and-groaners are a programming staple. Top attractions like Gorgeous George (pictured here) build a fanatical following with zany costumes and mannerisms.

John Cameron Swayze: His *Camel News Caravan* is the dominant news program of the era.

The Voice of Firestone: Howard Barlow conducts classical and semi-classical music. Despite a limited audience appeal, the show will survive until 1963.

1949
THE YEAR OF THE YOO-HOO

Through the open window, Molly calls to her friend, Mrs. Bloom, as Gertrude Berg's *The Goldbergs* comes to television. Loaded with ethnic warmth, the show repeats the success it enjoyed for many years in radio. . . . This is a vintage year for family comedies, foremost among them *One Man's Family, Mama* and *The Aldrich Family*. The first in a long line of idiotic fathers appears in the person of Chester A. Riley, as Jackie Gleason stars in *The Life of Riley*. . . . It's a banner year for variety shows, too. *The Admiral Broadway Revue* features Sid Caesar and Imogene Coca, and what becomes known as the Chicago School of Television emerges with the low-keyed hi-jinks of *Garroway at Large*. *The Ed Wynn Show* and *The Herb Shriner Show* display the comedy talents of their stars, and *Fireball Fun for All* is a showcase for the frenetic zanyisms of Olsen and Johnson. And that noted ukulele strummer brings in his second video effort, *Arthur Godfrey and His Friends*. . . . We get our first look at manned space flight, as *Captain Video* zooms in. And youngsters see another kind of creative fantasy in Paul Tripp's *Mr. I. Magination*. . . . Mike Stokey begins *Pantomime Quiz*, a series that will have numerous incarnations. . . . The acerbic wit of George S. Kaufman spices *This Is Show Business*. . . . Chiller fans greet the incoming *Suspense* and *Lights Out*, and for action there's *The Big Story*, *Man Against Crime* (Ralph Bellamy) and *Martin Kane, Private Eye*. . . . Paul Whiteman, Fred Waring and Kay Kyser tootle into view, as does Sammy Kaye's hokey *So You Want to Lead a Band*. Roberta Quinlan sings on *Especially for You*, and pianist-singer Bob Howard becomes the first Negro to have his own television show. . . . Toscanini conducts the NBC Symphony in November. . . . *Town Meeting of the Air* and *American Forum* illuminate the issues of the day. Human interest stories are the attractions on *We the People*. . . . For more specialized tastes: Dione Lucas does TV's first cooking show; Dennis James explains wrestling on *Okay, Mother*. . . . The year begins with the inauguration of Harry S. Truman, and when 1949 passes into history there are one million television sets in the land.

The Goldbergs: This show repeats the great success it enjoyed in radio, much of it due to Gertrude Berg's acting and script-writing prowess. Other family members: Philip Loeb as Jake, Eli Mintz as Uncle Dave, Arlene McQuade as Rosalie and Larry Robinson as Sammy.

29

1949

Captain Video: Al Hodge is the intrepid Captain in the show that sets the pattern for all the space-adventure epics to follow.

Godfrey and His Friends: The friends include Haleloke (shown here), Frank Parker, Marion Marlowe, the McGuire Sisters, Janette Davis and announcer Tony Marvin. One friend will get the heave-ho (on the air) in 1955 when Arthur Godfrey declares that singer Julius La Rosa "lacks humility."

1949

Dave Garroway: Shown here on the set of the Chicago-based *Garroway at Large*, he offers an easygoing brand of humor that contrasts vividly with the more frantic comedy found elsewhere on the dial. Other cast members: Jack Haskell, Cliff Norton, Connie Russell.

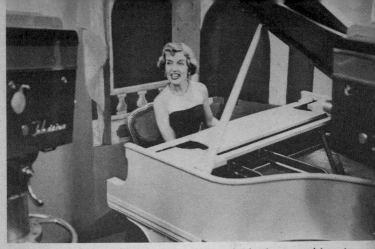

Roberta Quinlan: Her personality and singing combine to make her one of the best-known performers of TV's beginning years.

Ed Wynn: He's known as The Perfect Fool, and his visual comedy style makes his show a popular television attraction.

Martin Kane, Private Eye: William Gargan is one of four men who will play the lead role in various versions of this series (others: Lee Tracy, Lloyd Nolan, Mark Stevens).

Kraft Theatre: Shakespeare's "The Comedy of Errors" is presented in December 1949. Among the cast members are Harry Townes (lower left) and James Daly (upper right).

35

This Is Show Business: The gimmicky format of this show has contestants asking a panel of experts some semi-serious questions about the world of entertainment. Participants include (l.-r.) comic Sam Levenson, playwright George S. Kaufman, moderator Clifton Fadiman.

Mama: The trials and joys of the Hansens, this show sets a style in family comedy that will be much imitated in the years ahead. Peggy Wood, holding the cake, is Mama; the rest of the family (l.-r.) are Robin Morgan, Rosemary Rice, Dick Van Patten, Judson Laire and Ruth Gates.

Fred Waring: A radio favorite, he leads his Pennsylvanians into television on Easter Sunday of this year.

Arturo Toscanini: He conducts the NBC Symphony Orchestra when it makes the transition to television with occasional concerts.

Mary Hartline: The leader of the *Super Circus* band, she's the reason thousands of adult males are regular viewers of a kiddie show.

1950
THE YEAR OF THE NECKLINE

Television's first major controversy erupts this year. The burning issue: Are Miss Faye Emerson's gowns too revealing? The Great Cleavage Debate rages in the press briefly and then disappears. . . . There is intentional comedy too. Martin and Lewis are cavorting on *The Colgate Comedy Hour,* Jerry Lester and the statuesque Dagmar star on *Broadway Open House,* and *Four Star Revue* alternates Danny Thomas, Jack Carson, Jimmy Durante and Ed Wynn. Some household names in comedy begin their TV careers: Jack Benny, Burns and Allen, Ken Murray, Eddie Cantor, Bob Hope, Garry Moore (his is a daytime show). Caesar and Coca's opus is officially dubbed *Your Show of Shows* in 1950. . . . Art Linkletter's *Life with Linkletter* appears, as does that hardy perennial *The Arthur Murray Party.* . . . This year's flying objects are *Superman, Buck Rogers* and *Tom Corbett, Space Cadet.* . . . The new action series are *Rocky King, Detective* (Roscoe Karns), *Ellery Queen* and *Danger.* Gene Autry makes a galloping debut, and hard-boiled newspapermen are represented by *Big Town* and *I Cover Times Square.* . . . *Rootie Kazootie* and *Big Top* are beamed at the kids. Frank Sinatra makes his TV bow (on *Star Spangled Revue*). Perry Como gets his own show and Kate Smith makes her entrance. And *Your Hit Parade* begins its endless struggle to breathe new life into the same old pop songs each week. . . . A dozen new dramatic shows come on the air this year, notable among them *Lux Video Theatre* and *Robert Montgomery Presents.* . . . A soap opera, *The First Hundred Years,* begins its tearful journey. . . . Mark Goodson and Bill Todman launch *What's My Line?* and Groucho Marx lopes into video prominence with *You Bet Your Life.* Other panel and quiz first-timers: *Beat the Clock, Truth or Consequences, Life Begins at 80.* . . . Ethel Waters is a comedy maid in *Beulah,* Sherman Billingsley chats with the hoi polloi on *The Stork Club* and Renzo Cesana coos romantically through the candlelight as *The Continental.* . . . There are 4 million TV sets as television becomes a mass medium. . . . A transmitting tower goes up on the Empire State Building. . . . Charles Antell extols "Lanolin for the hair" and two dancing cigarette packs tap out the message that Old Golds are "made by tobacco men, not medicine men."

Faye Emerson: Her popular interview series runs for about three years. Here, she chats with William Cimilo, the "wayward bus driver", who left his Bronx route and drove to Miami.

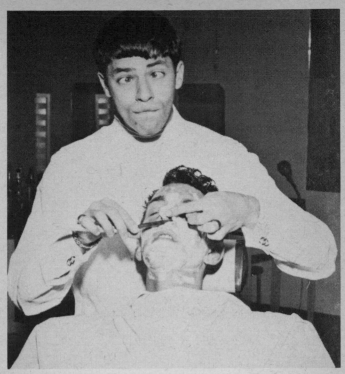

Martin and Lewis: Dean's drowsy baritone and Jerry's impish irreverence combine to form what many consider the perfect show-business team. The teamwork will end in an unfriendly parting in 1956; Lewis's success as a single will surprise no one, but few are prepared for Martin's subsequent popularity.

Your Show of Shows: Sid Caesar and Imogene Coca come into their own, backed by an awesome array of creative talent. Conceived by Pat Weaver, the show is produced by Max Liebman, and in the cast are Carl Reiner, Howard Morris, Marguerite Piazza; among the writers through the years are Mel Brooks, Woody Allen, Neil Simon, Lucille Kallen and Larry Gelbart. Here, guest Betty Furness (center) aids in the demolition of "A Streetcar Named Desire."

What's My Line?: The most enduringly popular of TV's panel shows (a syndicated version will still be running in the 1970's), its panel here is (l.-r.) Dorothy Kilgallen, Steve Allen, Arlene Francis and Bennett Cerf, with moderator John Daly.

You Bet Your Life: The emphasis is on comedy, as Groucho Marx (right, with announcer George Fenneman) launches his verbal darts in a quiz format. Also present: the Marx cigar and a stuffed duck ("Say the secret woid and the duck will give you a hundred dollars").

Life Begins at 80: The geriatric answer to *Juvenile Jury*, this panel show presents the wit and wisdom of the over-the-hill set. Here, regular Fred Stein observes guest Helen Clark.

Robert Montgomery Presents: Screen favorite Montgomery (shown with his daughter Elizabeth, of future *Bewitched* fame) begins a frequently acclaimed weekly dramatic series.

Helen Hayes: In the opening show of *Robert Montgomery Presents* she stars in "Victoria Regina."

Philco Playhouse: This 1950 performance of "Ann Rutledge" stars Stephen Courtleigh and Princess-to-be Grace Kelly.

Lux Video Theatre: A radio transplant, this series leans heavily on the marquee value of big-name performers. Here, Franchot Tone (right) stars with Claud Allister in ''Good-night Please.''

Little Women: This dramatization of the Louisa May Alcott novel features (l.-r.) June Dayton, Lois Steel, Mary Sinclair and Nancy Marchand, busy actresses in the dramatic shows of the Fifties.

Broadway Open House: The first of the late-night variety shows, it is emceed by comic Jerry Lester (at the outset, Morey Amsterdam alternates as host). Other regulars—Dagmar, Ray Malone, David Street, Wayne Howell and Milton DeLugg.

1950

Ken Murray: His brassy comedy-vaudeville show features Laurie Anders ("Ah love those waa-hd open spaces").

Garry Moore: He conducts a morning variety show stressing his offbeat, whimsical comedy. In the cast: announcer Durward Kirby, singers Ken Carson and Denise Lor.

Perry Como: The one-time Pennsylvania barber begins his own show after two years with *The Chesterfield Supper Club*. Viewers are charmed by his relaxed nonchalance.

Burns and Allen: Gracie's addled non sequiturs and George's air of amused tolerance come to TV after delighting radio and vaudeville audiences for years.

Superman: In this adaptation of the comic strip, George Reeves dons the gaudy union suit of the Man of Steel.

Rocky King, Detective: Roscoe Karns (right, with Walter Brooke) is a brains-over-brawn police lieutenant.

Tom Corbett, Space Cadet: Space fantasies are fast becoming a major segment of children's programming. This one stars Frankie Thomas.

53

Your Hit Parade: The week's tops in pops, decorated with some visual gingerbread. There will be numerous cast changes in the show's eight-year run; the early singers pictured here are (l.-r.) Dorothy Collins, Russell Arms, Gisele MacKenzie and Snooky Lanson.

The Arthur Murray Party: Vivacious Kathryn and stolid Arthur start a variety series that will run, off and on, into the Sixties. A more than incidental by-product of the show is the promotional build-up of the host's dance studios.

Boxing: It's a twice-a-week fixture on the sports fans' TV agenda, though television will later be blamed for killing off the small arenas and thus hastening boxing's decline. Friday's blow-by-blow commentator is Jimmy Powers (left). Wednesday's is Russ Hodges—with Bill the Bartender (Bill Nimmo) handling the beer commercials.

Stork Club: An impassive Sherman Billingsley interviews "the swells" in a TV replica of his night club.

Kate Smith: The Songbird of the South (shown with producer Ted Collins) starts her own music-and-talk series. The flower arrangement on the desk, a familiar sight in early television, provides camouflage for a hidden microphone.

The Continental: Suave actor Renzo Cesana murmurs sweet nothings to the females in the audience, thereby inducing sighs of rapture or uncontrollable laughter.

1951
THE YEAR OF THE NERVOUS HANDS

The lanky Senator from Tennessee, Estes Kefauver, is the central figure in dramatic hearings on organized crime. A spellbound America watches committee counsel Rudolph Halley grill fidgety underworld figures. . . . President Truman's address to the Japanese Peace Treaty Conference is the first coast-to-coast TV transmission, via coaxial cable. . . . The championship game of the National Football League is telecast for the first time, the DuMont Network paying $75,000 for the privilege. But the National Collegiate Athletic Association, fearing dwindling attendance at *its* games, bans unrestricted TV coverage. . . . Some noteworthy new dramatic series: *Goodyear Playhouse, Schlitz Playhouse* and *Celanese Theatre*. Charlton Heston plays Macbeth on *Studio One,* and Menotti's *Amahl and the Night Visitors* gets its initial airing. . . . Dinah Shore and James Melton have shows of their own, as does fiddler Florian ZaBach. . . . National audiences get their first look at an unconventional Philadelphian named Ernie Kovacs, an antic youngster named Steve Allen and a former burlesque comic named Pinky Lee. . . . *I Love Lucy,* which will become the most popular show in TV history, debuts—and loses its first sponsor, a tobacco company, because it just doesn't sell enough cigarettes. . . . Stu Erwin is the bewildered papa in *The Trouble with Father.* An all-Negro cast does *Amos 'n' Andy.* . . . 1951's action vehicles include *Mr. District Attorney, Mark Saber, Racket Squad, The Cisco Kid* and *Foreign Assignment* (later called *Foreign Intrigue*). . . . This year the kids get heroes transplanted from the comics (*Flash Gordon, Dick Tracy*) and more edifying fare (*Mr. Wizard, Zoo Parade*). . . . The heart-tugging *Strike It Rich* and the mind-boggling *You Asked for It* are among the new panel and game shows. Others: *Down You Go, Songs for Sale, The Name's the Same, It's News to Me.* . . . Edward R. Murrow's *See It Now* begins its illustrious career. . . . More than 10 million homes are equipped with the magic box, and some are tuned to a show (*Bride* and *Groom*) that provides, among the commercials, a free wedding service and a shower of gifts for the chosen couple. Other lovers (cigar category) hear a seductive pitch: "Why don't you pick me up and smoke me some time?"

Kefauver Hearings: One of the star witnesses is raspy-voiced gambler Frank Costello. He asks that his face not be photographed, and so the cameras focus relentlessly on the nervous movements of his hands.

President Truman: He is the first American President to receive extensive television coverage. Here, he greets Gen. Dwight Eisenhower, returning from a NATO inspection tour.

See It Now: Newsman Edward R. Murrow (partnered with producer Fred Friendly) begins a series of tough, provocative weekly half hours that will set a tone (and a standard) for the documentary form in the years to come.

1951

I Love Lucy: It debuts as just another wacky situation comedy, but it blossoms into a national institution. The inspired foolery of comedienne Lucille Ball (seated right) is the central ingredient, abetted by (l.-r.) William Frawley, Vivian Vance, husband Desi Arnaz. The show gains momentum as the years roll on, and will be rerun endlessly in the daytime by local stations.

Amos 'n' Andy: When this was radio's most popular show, two white men played the lead roles. In television, there's an all-Negro cast, with Johnny Lee (left) as Calhoun, and Tim Moore as The Kingfish (the leads are played by Alvin Childress and Spencer Williams). Almost 20 years later, there will be protests about the program's portrayal of blacks as comedy caricatures, and CBS will hastily withdraw it from syndication.

The Trouble with Father: One of the first of the well-meaning but semi-conscious father figures is played by Stu Erwin, with June Collyer as his long-suffering wife.

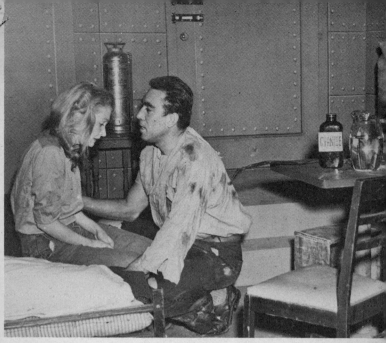

Lights Out: A suspense vehicle that flourished in radio doesn't do so well in TV. This 1951 episode, "The House of Dust," stars Nina Foch and Anthony Quinn.

Studio One: He's destined to be a movie headliner, but this year actor Charlton Heston is playing colonist James Otis in "A Bolt of Lightning."

1951

Ernie Kovacs: He comes to network television with an arsenal of electronic tricks, a bizarre sense of humor and a lovely foil (his wife, Edie Adams). His comedy characters and visual gimmickry are creative gems and, until his untimely death in 1962, he is acknowledged to be the most innovative and brilliant of the new television breed.

Sam Levenson: A Brooklyn schoolteacher turned storyteller, his show is the framework for bittersweet tales of an urban childhood.

Pinky Lee: An ex-burlesque comic, he stars in a musical-comedy series called *Those Two*, with Vivian Blaine.

Frank Sinatra: The young crooner has his own show, and the girls are still swooning. He's shown here with Rosemary Clooney, who appears on *Songs for Sale*.

Down You Go: A Chicago-based word game, its cast consists of (l.-r.) Carmelita Pope, moderator Dr. Bergen Evans, Toni Gilman and (not shown) Robert Breen and Francis Coughlin.

You Asked for It: At the request of viewers, host Art Baker presents a grab-bag assortment of people and events. He's shown with Willamary, one of the world's few professional theremin soloists.

Strike It Rich: Contestants pour out tales of personal tragedy as they compete for prizes. Here, emcee Warren Hull is shorn by a lady barber.

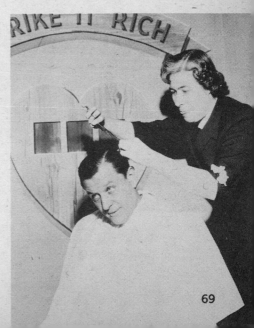

Mr. District Attorney: Jay Jostyn protects the public weal in the lead role, as he did in the radio version.

Mark Saber: When this series begins, it is titled *Mystery Theater* and Saber (Tom Conway) is with the homicide squad. In a second go-round for the show, Saber has other duties; in its third, and final, version (1957) the lead will be played by Donald Gray.

Racket Squad: Reed Hadley, as Captain Braddock (the pretty villainess is Hillary Brooke), unmasks swindlers and con artists.

The Cisco Kid: Duncan Renaldo (left) is the Kid; Leo Carillo is his sidekick, Pancho.

1952
THE YEAR OF THE POLITE COP

"All we want are the facts, ma'am." The flat, unemotional voice belongs to *Dragnet*'s Sgt. Joe Friday, and Jack Webb's terse underplaying will be much imitated in the years ahead. . . . 1952's other new action series are more traditional: *Gangbusters, Boston Blackie* and *Dangerous Assignment*. . . . General Eisenhower makes extensive use of television in his campaign for the Presidency ("I shall go to Korea"). And his embattled running mate, Richard Nixon, uses the medium for his "Checkers" speech. . . . This is a year of innovation. With Dave Garroway at the helm, the *Today* show (brainchild of Sylvester Weaver) comes on the air; *Omnibus* bows; Bishop Fulton Sheen goes on opposite Milton Berle; educational TV arrives; the Kentucky Derby is telecast live. . . . On *This Is Show Business*, George S. Kaufman protests the commercialization of Christmas, saying "Let's make this one program on which no one sings 'Silent Night.'" Protests roll in and Kaufman is suspended, then reinstated. . . . Goodson and Todman launch another panel favorite, *I've Got a Secret,* and the guessing games multiply, with the mink-swathed *Big Payoff*, the erudite *Information Please* and the makeup man's delight, *Masquerade Party*. . . . A deluge of situation comedies descends: *Mr. Peepers* (Wally Cox), *Our Miss Brooks* (Eve Arden), *My Friend Irma* (Marie Wilson), *My Little Margie* (Gale Storm), *My Hero* (Robert Cummings), *Meet Millie* (Elena Verdugo), *I Married Joan* (Joan Davis), *Life with Luigi* (J. Carrol Naish), *Ozzie and Harriet* (Ozzie and Harriet). . . . Liberace, previously a syndicated phenomenon, goes network. . . . Jackie Gleason gets his own show, and so does a young comic named Red Buttons, who sings "Strange things are happening." Jack Paar labors in obscurity as the host of *I've Got News for You*. . . . Muffled sobs are heard throughout the land as Ralph Edwards opens his book and intones, "This is your life." . . . Walter Winchell starts the television version of his radio newcast. . . . *Victory at Sea* is launched. . . . Dr. Frances Horwich beams *Ding Dong School* at pre-schoolers. . . . More than 15 million American families are now huddled around the wonderful watching machine, to be told, "Bufferin acts twice as fast as aspirin," and asked, "How are you fixed for blades?"

Dragnet: Joe Friday and Frank Smith (Jack Webb and Ben Alexander, l.-r.) are unfailingly polite in their pursuit of malefactors. The show meticulously reproduces police methods and jargon, and it sympathetically portrays the cop as a hardworking (often overworked) public servant.

Jackie Gleason: After a stint as Chester A. Riley, Gleason gets his own comedy show. Most popular segment is a sketch called "The Honeymooners," with Gleason as bus driver Ralph Kramden, Art Carney as sewer worker Ed Norton, and Audrey Meadows (shown here) and Joyce Randolph as their wives.

Red Buttons: With comedy experience in the Catskill resorts and on the burlesque stage, Buttons brings a fresh and appealing style to TV. His first season is a triumph, but the bubble will burst the following year and the show will disappear in 1954 despite the rescue efforts of a platoon of writers.

Omnibus: It's a melange of music, dance, comedy, drama and information presented by producer Robert Saudek and introduced by the urbane host, Alistair Cooke (pictured). It will appear on all three networks in the course of its lengthy run, and among other memorable moments we'll see the TV debut of Nichols and May, Orson Welles playing Lear, Frank Lloyd Wright expounding on architecture, Saroyan explaining Saroyan.

Walter Winchell: The veteran gossip columnist makes no concessions to the new medium; his old radio news show is virtually unchanged when he moves before the cameras with his jaunty fedora, staccato delivery and breathless "scoops."

1952

Bishop Sheen: The program is called *Life Is Worth Living* and it consists of an educational/inspirational talk by Bishop Fulton J. Sheen. It is the only religious series ever programmed weekly in prime time, and the Bishop's charisma will attract a large and loyal audience for five consecutive seasons.

Today: News and interviews in the early morning? They said it couldn't be done, but this show does it, surviving a shaky start and some critical blasts. The original cast, grouped with chimpanzee J. Fred Muggs, includes (l.-r.) newsman Frank Blair, anchorman Dave Garroway, announcer Jack Lescoulie.

Ozzie and Harriet: The Nelson family includes (l.-r.) mother Harriet, sons Ricky and David, father Ozzie. A family comedy carried over from radio, *Ozzie and Harriet* achieves even greater popularity in TV.

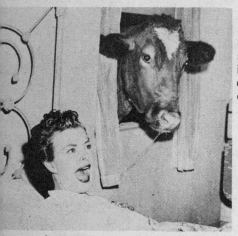

My Little Margie: Gale Storm stars in a raucous, slapstick situation comedy that is destined to grind on forever in syndication.

I Married Joan: There's not much subtlety, but co-stars Joan Davis and Jim Backus provide plenty of laughs in this situation comedy.

78

1952

Mr. Peepers: Wally Cox (shown here with Patricia Benoit) is a shy, small-town junior-high-school teacher. Deftly written, *Mr. Peepers* is a warm and poignant comedy that's a cut above others of this genre. Also in the cast: Tony Randall, Marion Lorne, Georgann Johnson.

My Friend Irma: Marie Wilson (foreground) plays the featherbrained Irma, and Cathy Lewis is her patient friend Jane.

79

Liberace: A genuine phenomenon makes its network debut in 1952. Liberace has curly hair, nimble fingers and what seems like millions of sparkling teeth. He keeps a candelabra on his piano and, while his brother George (left) fiddles discreetly in the background, he wallops out shmaltzy renditions of all sorts of tunes. For millions of women, especially the middle-aged, he becomes an overnight culture hero.

I've Got a Secret: No one cares much about the flimsy "secrets" of the guests; the show's popularity derives from the reactions and comments of the panel—(seated, l.-r.) Jayne Meadows, Henry Morgan and Faye Emerson—and moderator Garry Moore.

This Is Your Life: Ralph Edwards snares unwary celebrities and parades their past life before the cameras in a manner that is sometimes touching and often mawkish. Here, he surprises Dr. Lee De Forest (right).

Olympic Telethon: Bob Hope (left) and Bing Crosby, becoming more and more active in TV, appear together this year on a telethon, to raise money for American participation in the Helsinki Olympic Games.

Victory at Sea: It is TV's first historical documentary series and remains one of its best. It re-creates the naval war in the Pacific, with a score by Richard Rodgers.

1953

THE YEAR OF THE BASHFUL BUTCHER

"Whadaya wanna do tonight, Marty?" The words are by Paddy Chayefsky, and his drama about a Bronx misfit (played by Rod Steiger) becomes the most memorable in TV annals. . . . "Memorable" is the word for several other 1953 events: the coronation of Elizabeth II is telecast; viewers see an A-bomb test, live, from Yucca Flats, Nev.; the *Ford 50th Anniversary Show,* shown simultaneously on NBC and CBS, becomes a landmark in TV entertainment, with its greatest moment a medley by Mary Martin and Ethel Merman. . . . Edward R. Murrow steps out of his newsman's role to interview celebrities on *Person to Person,* and Walter Cronkite follows suit as narrator of *You Are There.* . . . This is the year when many movie and stage stars decide they'd rather switch than fight. Danny Thomas begins a long run in *Make Room for Daddy.* Ray Bolger is in *Where's Raymond?,* Ray Milland in *Meet Mr. McNutley,* Ezio Pinza in *Bonino,* Ann Sothern in *Private Secretary.* . . . *Topper* and *Life with Father* both get TV treatments. So do Clem Kaddiddlehopper and the Mean Widdle Kid, as *The Red Skelton Show* debuts. . . . A curiosity of the season is *Action in the Afternoon.* It's a Western telecast from an unlikely frontier town—Philadelphia. . . . Jack Paar, still warming up for his big moment, is host of a quiz show titled *Bank on the Stars.* Fred Allen, unable to duplicate his radio success in television, presides over *Judge for Yourself.* Other 1953 game shows: *Double or Nothing, Name That Tune, Place the Face, Dr. I.Q.* and Peter Potter's ("Will it be a hit—*bong*—or a miss—*clunk?*") *Jukebox Jury.* . . . The year's drama comes in oddly assorted packages. There's the often distinguished *U.S. Steel Hour;* the low-budget, high-creativity *Camera Three;* and *G.E. Theater,* with Ronald Reagan, the future Governor of California, as host ("I don't see him as Governor," someone will wisecrack. "He's more the Best Friend type."). Loretta Young, resplendent in spectacular gowns, delivers *A Letter to Loretta;* and Adolphe Menjou, equally natty, introduces *My Favorite Story.* . . . Milton Berle, slipping in the ratings, switches to situation comedy. . . . In 20 million television homes Speedy Alka-Seltzer fights stomach upset and Bardahl battles Dirty Sludge and Blackie Carbon.

Marty: A superb performance by Rod Steiger in the title role (here dancing with Nancy Marchand) helps make this play a classic among the realistic dramas that flourish in the Fifties. In the later movie version, Ernest Borgnine will win an Academy Award for his portrayal of the nebbish butcher.

Ford Fiftieth Anniversary Show: This lavish special becomes the pacesetting model for the hundreds that will follow in the years ahead. It is produced by Leland Hayward, with a cast including Edward R. Murrow, Marian Anderson, Oscar Hammerstein II, Amos 'n' Andy, Ollie Dragon. And, though the stools-on-a-bare-stage setting will be much imitated, the chemistry of the Mary Martin-Ethel Merman duet proves inimitable.

Amahl and the Night Visitors: Gian Carlo Menotti's perennial Christmas opera was first shown in 1951; it is restaged this year with Rosemary Kuhlmann and Bill McIver as the mother and son.

Loretta Young: She makes her entrances in a swirl of chic finery, then introduces (and occasionally performs in) half-hour playlets.

General Electric Theater: Ronald Reagan is the host and a frequent performer in this drama series (he's shown here in "The Orphans"). The show will also prove helpful in Reagan's subsequent political ventures, since it improves what the experts call "the recognition factor."

1953

Hamlet: Maurice Evans, who will become television's foremost Shakespearean actor, makes his TV debut on this *Hallmark Hall of Fame* (also making *its* debut) interpretation of the classic. Also in the cast: Ruth Chatterton, Joseph Schildkraut and Sarah Churchill.

Studio One: This play, "Dry Run," stars Katherine McLeod and Walter Matthau in a tale of derring-do aboard a World War II submarine.

Kraft Theatre: The first drama show to be colorcast is "To Live in Peace," with Jerome Kilty and Judith Braun.

Rip Van Winkle: A bewhiskered E. G. Marshall plays Rip in this *Kraft Theatre* Christmas offering. He's shown here with Mary Johnson and Lon Brown.

91

1953

Private Secretary: Fun at the office, with Ann Sothern as secretary Susie MacNamara.

My Favorite Husband: This sitcom stars Barry Nelson and Joan Caulfield (later replaced by Vanessa Brown).

92

The Life of Riley: William Bendix becomes the lamebrained Riley; in the 1949 version Jackie Gleason played the role.

Make Room for Daddy: Night-club performer Danny Thomas plays a night-club performer (shown here with Rusty Hamer). Also in the cast: Marjorie Lord (succeeded later by Jean Hagen), Jesse White, Sherry Jackson.

93

Red Skelton: His show's huge success will spring from Skelton's portrayal of a gallery of comedy characters. A gifted pantomimist, Skelton uses pathos as well as slapstick.

Eddie Fisher: Just out of the Army, the young singer stars in the 15-minute *Coke Time*, twice weekly.

1953

Jack Paar: With the golden days yet to come, this year finds Paar doing a morning variety show and a summer quizzer. Singer Betty Clooney and bandleader Pupi Campo are in the variety cast.

Colgate Comedy Hour: A versatile performer, Donald O'Connor often stars in this variety series. He's shown with sidekick Sidney Miller (at the piano) in their popular songwriters sketch.

Dollar a Second: It's a quiz show, but the brash comedy of Jan Murray (shown here with a contestant) overshadows the questions and answers.

I Led Three Lives: Herbert Philbrick's book about Communist subversion is the source of this counterspy saga. Richard Carlson plays Philbrick.

1953

Action in the Afternoon: Jack Valentine is the star of the only Western ever to be telecast from Philadelphia.

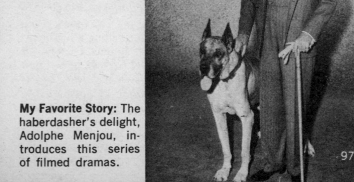

My Favorite Story: The haberdasher's delight, Adolphe Menjou, introduces this series of filmed dramas.

97

1954
THE YEAR OF THE POINT OF ORDER

It's a casting director's dream. There's Sen. Joe McCarthy, feared by some, revered by others. There's the courtly little Boston lawyer, Joseph Welch ("At long last, sir, have you no sense of decency?"). There are the intrepid investigators, Cohn and Schine. And there is an obviously rattled Secretary of the Army. The televised Army–McCarthy Hearings drag on inconclusively, but it is generally agreed that this public exposure signals the downfall of the Wisconsin Senator. . . . 1954 is a year of "Happenings." The world's two greatest milers, Roger Bannister and John Landy, meet in a match race. In full view of millions, Jackie Gleason races offstage and breaks his leg. . . . The Miss America Pageant is telecast for the first time. . . . Leonard Bernstein launches a TV career when he explains Beethoven on *Omnibus*. . . . Steve Allen takes over *The Tonight Show*. Arlene Francis is the central figure of an ambitious daily program for women, *Home*. Attempting to counter NBC's successful *Today* show, CBS hatches *The Morning Show* (with Walter Cronkite). It fails. . . . TV's first "spectacular" is a spectacular failure too. Max Liebman's "Satins and Spurs," costing a purported $300,-000, is savaged by the critics. But the concept of lavish specials is here to stay. . . . All three networks carry "The Diamond Jubilee of Light," and the show is stolen by a young comedian named George Gobel. . . . Reginald Rose's "Twelve Angry Men" is on *Studio One*, as original drama flourishes. . . . Lawyers dominate two new series—*Justice* and *Public Defender*. But doctors are better served by a realistic new show, *Medic*. . . . The sitcoms keep coming—*Father Knows Best* (Robert Young), *December Bride* (Spring Byington), *Halls of Ivy* (Ronald Colman), etc. . . . Still awaiting a big break, Jack Paar has a daytime variety series, Johnny Carson asks questions on *Earn Your Vacation*, Ernie Kovacs runs a quiz show called *Time Will Tell*. . . . *Disneyland* is here. So are the dog days, as *Lassie* and *Rin Tin Tin* both come woofing into television. . . . A sudsy drama, *The Secret Storm*, begins a run that will still continue nearly two decades later. . . . 26 million homes now have TV sets, and they see Betty Furness extolling the virtues of a refrigerator and a penguin nagging them to "Switch from hots to Kools!"

Army-McCarthy Hearings: An era of fear and suspicion reaches a climax in a Senate hearing room, while the nation watches on television. The Communist-hunting Sen. Joseph McCarthy ("Who promoted Peress?") and his tactics ("Point of order!") receive protracted national exposure, and many viewers do not like what they see. The hearings will lead to McCarthy's condemnation by his Senate colleagues, and his political star will continue to decline until his death in 1957.

Satins and Spurs: It's an original musical comedy, produced by Max Liebman and starring Betty Hutton. Ballyhooed as TV's first "spectacular," it fails to live up to the press agentry, but the concept of the "special" show will survive.

Producer's Showcase: A monthly series of 90-minute dramas, its premiere is "Three by Coward," which is produced and directed by Otto Preminger—here flanked by Gloria Vanderbilt (left) and Ginger Rogers, both making their TV debuts.

Leonard Bernstein: The young conductor of the New York Philharmonic begins a long TV career when he appears on *Omnibus* to talk about Beethoven's Fifth Symphony.

101

Twelve Angry Men: A *Studio One* jury-room drama by Reginald Rose, it achieves renown as one of television's best. In the cast: Franchot Tone, Robert Cummings, Edward Arnold, Walter Abel, Paul Hartman, Norman Fell.

Arrowsmith: This dramatization of the Sinclair Lewis novel appears on *Kraft Theatre*, with Richard Kiley starring.

Burlesque: 1954 is a year of exceptional dramas, and this is one of them. It stars Art Carney (left, with his brother Fred Carney, who directs it).

Climax!: Live Drama is still the thing when this Hollywood-based series begins (eventually it will be filmed). The premiere telecast (pictured) is Raymond Chandler's "The Long Goodbye," starring Dick Powell and Teresa Wright.

Ford Theatre: The offerings in this series have an uneven quality, but there are plenty of stars to attract viewers. Pictured here are Jack Lemmon and Ida Lupino in a comedy titled "Marriageable Male."

Medic: Realistic medical dramas, they're produced by Worthington Miner and written by James Moser. Richard Boone achieves stardom in the role of Dr. Konrad Styner.

Tonight: After a year as a local show in New York, this late-night variety series goes network in 1954. Steve Allen is the star (he's shown with bandleader Skitch Henderson) and he's supported by Gene Rayburn, Steve Lawrence, Eydie Gorme and Andy Williams.

Home: Another Pat Weaver idea, this "magazine" for women has Arlene Francis as its editor-in-chief, assisted by Hugh Downs. Although it will run for more than three years, the concept of meaningful daytime programming is perhaps ahead of its time.

1954

Disneyland: The Walt Disney empire is extended to television with this weekly potpourri of cartoons and films, old and new, introduced by Disney himself.

People Are Funny: Art Linkletter goads willing contestants through some outlandish stunts. Here, Linkletter presents $20,000 to Dorilla Dufresne and Bill Harper, a couple brought together by Univac.

Lassie: The cast, including the star bow-wow, will change in the years ahead, but youngsters continue to be fascinated with these stories of a courageous collie. The original family includes (l.-r.) George Cleveland, Jan Clayton and Tommy Rettig.

Rin Tin Tin: These canine adventures are set in Fort Apache, with a German shepherd in the lead role. Co-starring are Jim L. Brown (left) and Lee Aaker.

Father Knows Best: Though it's dropped by its first sponsor after an initial 26-week run, this Middle American comedy goes on to attain enormous popularity. The Anderson family, here grouped around father Jim (Robert Young), consists of (l.-r.) Billy Gray, Elinor Donahue, Jane Wyatt and Lauren Chapin.

December Bride: Love, senior-citizen style. It stars Spring Byington (left, with Verna Felton and Will Wright).

109

Betty Furness: Her commercials for home appliances always have the tag line "You can be sure if it's Westinghouse."

The Morning Show: CBS attempts to compete with the NBC's *Today*. The cast includes (l.-r.) Charles Collingwood, puppeteers Bil and Cora Baird, Walter Cronkite.

Landy-Bannister Race: This is the Dream Race, a match between the only two men who can run the mile in less than four minutes. It is televised from Vancouver, B.C., and Roger Bannister (pictured) edges John Landy in 3:58.8.

1955
THE YEAR OF THE SIX-GUN

The arrival in September of *The Life and Legend of Wyatt Earp* and, four days later, *Gunsmoke,* marks the beginning of an "adult Western" trend that will eventually stampede television. . . . Another, more ominous, trend is gathering momentum: the big-money quiz show is here, as *The $64,000 Question* makes its debut. . . . Perry Como moves in opposite Jackie Gleason and reduces The Fat One's fat Saturday-night ratings. . . . *See It Now,* a weekly fixture since 1951, is cut back to occasional specials. . . . Mary Martin soars into TV history as "Peter Pan," attracting the largest audience to date —65 million viewers. . . . Other outstanding adaptations include "The Caine Mutiny Court-Martial," "The Skin of Our Teeth," "The Petrified Forest" (with Humphrey Bogart making his only TV dramatic appearance), "Darkness at Noon" (with Lee J. Cobb) and a musical version of "Our Town" (with Paul Newman, Eva Marie Saint and Frank Sinatra— singing "Love and Marriage"). . . . Top originals of 1955: Rod Serling's "Patterns," Gore Vidal's "Visit to a Small Planet" and James Costigan's "A Wind from the South." . . . Among the new weekly entries are a comedy about a con man in khaki, *You'll Never Get Rich* (known to one and all as "the Bilko show"); a musical bubble-maker, *The Lawrence Welk Show;* and a technological tour de force, *Wide Wide World.* For the kids, there's *Captain Kangaroo, The Mickey Mouse Club* and *Disneyland*'s "Davy Crockett." Other arrivals of 1955: *The Millionaire, Captain Gallant, Grand Ole Opry, Ethel and Albert, Robin Hood, Romper Room, Sgt. Preston of the Yukon, Matinee Theatre.* . . . Audiences see a President spar with the press for the first time, as Eisenhower consents to have his news conferences filmed for TV. . . . Judy Garland makes her TV debut. Julius La Rosa makes a sudden exit—fired on the air by Arthur Godfrey. . . . Movies get their first foothold in network TV, as ABC buys 100 films from J. Arthur Rank for *Afternoon Film Festival.* . . . *Project 20* is launched, with "Nightmare in Red." . . . Oscar ceremonies are telecast for the first time. . . . Bert and Harry are selling beer, Commander Whitehead is pushing "Schweppervescence" and the cigarette preferred by cowboys has "filter, flavor, flip-top box."

Gunsmoke: The play, not the gunplay, is the thing. Characterizations are developed in some depth, and all sorts of themes are woven into the storylines of this indestructible Western. James Arness is Marshal Matt Dillon and the cast includes Amanda Blake, Dennis Weaver and Milburn Stone.

The Life and Legend of Wyatt Earp: Historians will say there's more legend than life in these tales about a frontier marshal, but audiences eagerly accept the show's attempt to stress character and ''realism'' rather than incessant shoot-outs. An unknown actor named Hugh O'Brian is propelled to fame in the title role (he's shown here with Faye Baker).

1955

Davy Crockett: Fess Parker is the frontiersman on three *Disneyland* installments, each an hour long. The shows catch the fancy of the young, and soon coonskin caps are selling in novelty stores everywhere.

Mickey Mouse Club: Another offshoot of the Disney empire, this daytimer features mouse ears and a club song. Here, Jimmie Dodd (center) leads the vocalizing.

The Elgin Hour: This is one of the many drama anthologies so prevalent in television in the Fifties. Here, Kim Stanley stars in "The Bridge."

Patterns: Rod Serling's brilliant drama about the ruthless executive politics of a large corporation is presented on *Kraft Theatre*. Richard Kiley (left) and Everett Sloane have the leads.

A Man Is Ten Feet Tall:
Though it will lose out
to "Patterns" in the
Emmy race, this orig-
inal teleplay by Robert
Alan Aurthur is stun-
ningly effective. Its
stars are (l.-r.) Martin
Balsam, Don Murray
and Sidney Poitier.

A Wind from the South:
Julie Harris stars in
James Costigan's sen-
sitive story about pre-
sent-day Ireland.

117

Peter Pan: James Barrie's fantasy gets a superlative TV production from Jerome Robbins, and its ecstatic reception makes it a candidate for endless repeats in the years ahead. Mary Martin is an effervescent Peter (here, she sings "I've Gotta Crow" with Heller Halliday) and Cyril Ritchard is Captain Hook.

You'll Never Get Rich: Phil Silvers (shown here with Alan Melvin—left—and Harvey Lembeck) is M/Sgt. Ernie Bilko in this Nat Hiken creation about a lovable schemer. Until its demise in 1959, the show will abound in comedy cameos by veteran performers like Paul Ford, Maurice Gosfield, Herbie Faye and Billy Sands.

The Caine Mutiny Court-Martial: Lloyd Nolan (right) and Barry Sullivan repeat their Broadway roles in the television version of the Pulitzer Prize play.

The Skin of Our Teeth: This adaptation of Thornton Wilder's comedy stars Mary Martin and George Abbott.

Cyrano de Bergerac: Jose Ferrer, who has often portrayed Cyrano, is the banana-nosed hero again in 1955 in this TV adaptation of Rostand's play.

Humphrey Bogart: The play is "The Petrified Forest" (here Bogart rehearses with wife Lauren Bacall) and it's the only television appearance this movie star will make.

Matinee Theatre: Hour-long daytime drama, five days a week, is supervised by producer Albert McCleery. It's a valiant effort that will last three seasons. Here (l.-r.), Charles Macaulay, Natalie Norwich, Peggy Weber and Richard Boone appear in "Wuthering Heights."

James Dean: He will go on to become a world-famous screen star, but he is still an unknown when he appears in this 1955 play (with Pat Hardy) called "The Unlighted Road," on *Schlitz Playhouse of Stars.*

Four Star Playhouse: Charles Boyer, Dick Powell, Rosalind Russell and Joel McCrea were the original quartet, but by 1955 it's a threesome comprising Powell, Boyer and David Niven. Here, Niven stars in "Here Comes the Suit."

123

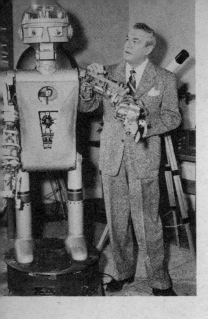

Science Fiction Theatre: Syndicated weirdness, with Truman Bradley narrating (here he holds hands with one episode's leading character).

Shock Theater: This year's quirky innovation is the ghoulish host who comments on old horror films. In the East there's Zacherley (here peering over a cauliflower "brain") and on the West Coast there's a young lady known as Vampira.

Alfred Hitchcock Presents: Each macabre playlet is preceded by a perversely witty monologue, delivered deadpan by Hitchcock. And each is followed by an epilogue in which the director assures viewers that crime doesn't pay, a point seldom made clear in the plays themselves.

125

The Millionaire: A mysterious billionaire doles out million-dollar checks; Marvin Miller (pictured) plays the courier. It's all make-believe, but thousands of viewers write in, pleading for a share of the largesse.

Highway Patrol: This syndicated action series is all over the dials, with Broderick Crawford growling "Ten-four" when he completes his calls to headquarters.

Godfrey-LaRosa: Young singer Julius LaRosa (left) is one of the friends on *Godfrey and His Friends* until, publicly and without warning, he is bounced by the boss because he "lacks humility."

Martha Raye: After guest appearances on almost every variety show in sight, the comedienne got her own show in 1953, and it runs sporadically through four seasons. Ex-champ Rocky Graziano is her comedy foil and in the 1955 scene shown here, her guest (right) is Margaret Truman.

Johnny Carson: He has a morning variety show in the summer of this year. Few realize what lies ahead for him.

Lawrence Welk: He speaks with an accent, the music is ricky-tick, and there are "Mickey Mouse" gimmicks like floating bubbles and a Champagne Lady. But bandleader Welk (shown with Champagne Lady Alice Lon) has found a magic formula that appeals to the middle-aged-and-upwards set, and the band plays on—and on (almost 20 years later, the show will get a fresh start in syndication).

129

The $64,000 Question: In radio the top prize was only $64 and now the ante (and the excitement) is increased a thousandfold. Suspense builds as contestants try to answer questions that increase in value and difficulty. Here, hostess Lynn Dollar steers a contestant, Lt. John von Rueden, toward emcee Hal March.

The $100,000 Big Surprise: It seems that big-money prizes mean big ratings, and the rush is on. Mike Wallace emcees this one.

1956
THE YEAR OF THE HEAVYWEIGHT

It is the second show in a new dramatic series called *Playhouse 90,* and it's a blockbuster. The play is Rod Serling's "Requiem for a Heavyweight," the story of a washed-up prizefighter. Jack Palance is the pathetic Mountain McClintock, with Kim Hunter, Ed Wynn and Keenan Wynn in sharply etched supporting roles. . . . 1956 has other dramatic highlights: an emotional performance by Lloyd Bridges in "Tragedy in a Temporary Town," an adaptation of John Kennedy's book "Profiles in Courage," "A Night to Remember" and "Eloise." . . . The year also brings: "Out of Darkness," a chilling documentary on mental illness; the first TV showing of "The Wizard of Oz"; "The Secret Life of Danny Kaye," the comedian's UNESCO tour; Sonja Henie in "Holiday on Ice"; Frank Baxter narrating "Our Mr. Sun" in the *Bell Science Series;* the real-life drama of Grace Kelly's marriage to her handsome prince. . . . Royalty is seen in another light when the Duke and Duchess of Windsor appear on *Person to Person.* A bemused audience watches the Duchess demonstrate her proficiency in the game of jacks. . . . Ed Sullivan lands Elvis Presley as a guest star and CBS decrees that the cameras must sedately stay above the waist and ignore the hip-wriggling. . . . Huntley and Brinkley team up. Martin and Lewis split up. . . . NBC parts ways with its innovative president, Pat Weaver. . . . The rumors that *The $64,000 Question* is rigged are denied vehemently, and the big-money quiz boom continues with the debuts of *Twenty-One* and *The $64,000 Challenge.* . . . More new guessing games: *To Tell the Truth, The Price Is Right, Do You Trust Your Wife?* . . . Contestants spin tales of woe on *Queen for a Day.* . . . Woe befalls Buddy Hackett in an ill-fated series called *Stanley*, and Wally Cox with *The Adventures of Hiram Holliday.* . . . Walter Winchell, an old-time hoofer, starts a variety series, as does newcomer Tennessee Ernie Ford. . . . Clint Walker moseys into prominence with *Cheyenne.* . . . Most live shows are replaced by film, and the rush is on to buy post-1948 movies. . . . These slogans bombard the nation's 35 million TV homes: "You'll wonder where the yellow went," "*Leave* the driving to us" and "Winston tastes good, like a (*clap, clap*) cigarette should."

Requiem for a Heavyweight: One day people will look back on television of the 1950's and dub it The Golden Age of Drama; this play is one of the reasons. Rod Serling's script painfully probes the heights and depths of human relationships, and outstanding performances by (l.-r.) Keenan Wynn, Jack Palance and Ed Wynn make the words come to life.

133

A Night to Remember: Director George Roy Hill re-creates the sinking of the Titanic. It's done live, using seven cameras, 31 sets and 107 actors; though it's a staggering technical achievement, the production will be repeated just 35 days later.

Born Yesterday: Garson Kanin's comedy has Mary Martin as the giddy Billie Dawn and Arthur Hill as the reluctant tutor.

Dodsworth: An adaptation of the Sinclair Lewis novel, it stars Fredrick March with Claire Trevor and Geraldine Fitzgerald.

Cradle Song: An impressive cast is assembled for this Maurice Evans production on *Hallmark Hall of Fame:* Judith Anderson (not shown) and (l.-r.) Anthony Franciosa, Susan Strasberg, Siobhan McKenna and Helen Hayes.

Eloise: Kay Thompson's story about a little girl loose in the Plaza Hotel becomes an overproduced *Playhouse 90* venture starring Evelyn Rudie.

135

The Wizard of Oz: In 1956 kids get to see, via television, the film that charmed their parents in theaters. In this scene are (l.-r.) Ray Bolger, Jack Haley and Judy Garland.

Richard III: A motion picture starring Laurence Olivier and Claire Bloom, it's presented as a three-hour colorcast on *Wide Wide World*.

1956

Twentieth Century: The boisterous farce by Ben Hecht and Charles MacArthur stars Orson Welles as the bankrupt Broadway producer and Betty Grable as his leading lady.

Jack and the Beanstalk: The children's fable is turned into a musical with (l.-r.) Billy Gilbert, Celeste Holm and Joel Grey.

137

Huntley-Brinkley: They are experienced but unknown news-men when NBC teams them for the 1956 political conventions. Their amiable chatter is a welcome change of pace for viewers, and they are rewarded with a nightly 15-minute news show.

Out of Darkness: A remarkable study of mental illness, it's written and produced by Albert Wasserman, with narration by Orson Welles. The cameras study this woman, Doris L., throughout the course of her treatment.

The Twisted Cross: A *Project 20* documentary charting the rise and fall of Nazi Germany. Here Joseph Goebbels harangues a crowd of early Storm Troopers.

139

On Trial!: Some well-known performers appear in these courtroom dramas. This episode, "The De Santre Affair," stars Joan Fontaine.

Passport to Danger: Cesar Romero is a "trouble-shooting diplomatic courier" in this syndicated series.

Cheyenne: Clint Walker plays Cheyenne Bodie, a phlegmatic frontier scout, in this popular "adult Western."

Jane Wyman Theater: Miss Wyman introduces the plays in this series and appears in some of them. Here, she is a concert pianist in "Sound of Thunder."

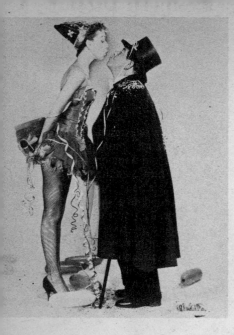

Stanley: Despite the talent of the young comedy leads (Buddy Hackett and Carol Burnett), this series expires after one season.

142

Elvis Presley: The rock-'n'-roll idol's top half is seen on *The Ed Sullivan Show*, as cameras discreetly aim above his waist.

1956

The Price Is Right: Big prizes for contestants who can guess the price of merchandise. Bill Cullen dispenses the boodle.

Queen for a Day: Women vie for the crown by telling hard-luck stories. The audience selects the winner and Jack Bailey rewards her with gifts of assorted merchandise.

143

1957
THE YEAR OF THE TALK SHOW

The art of conversation (TV style) takes on a new dimension as Jack Paar becomes host of *The Tonight Show*. Nervous and emotional, Paar is nevertheless a brilliant conversationalist, and he introduces many new faces to television (among them: Alexander King, Elsa Maxwell, Dody Goodman). He also feuds openly with columnists and once, in a fit of pique, walks off his own show. Audiences love Paar's unpredictable style. . . . Mike Wallace goes network with his sensation-seeking interview show and one guest, mobster Mickey Cohen, uses the time to bad-mouth the Los Angeles police. . . . Cameras follow two distinguished visitors in 1957: Britain's Queen Elizabeth and Russia's volatile Nikita Khrushchev. . . . In a blaze of self-promotion, producer Mike Todd throws a televised party for himself in Madison Square Garden. Viewers of the garish spectacle miss a fine production of "Green Pastures," on another network. . . . Big names and big dramatic shows highlight this year: Julie Harris in "The Lark," Julie Andrews in "Cinderella," Lunt and Fontanne in "The Great Sebastians," Anne Bancroft in "The Miracle Worker," Charles Boyer and Katharine Cornell in "There Shall Be No Night." On *Studio One* Ralph Bellamy, William Shatner and Steve McQueen star in a two-parter called "The Defender," later to become a (pluralized) series. . . . Another defender, *Perry Mason* (Raymond Burr), is a big hit with the Nielsen jury. . . . 1957's sagebrush biggies are *Wagon Train, Have Gun, Will Travel* and *Maverick*. . . . Sitcom standouts are the hayseed *Real McCoys*, the sophisticated *Thin Man*, and the charming *Leave It to Beaver*. . . . Nat King Cole, sponsorless, lasts only one season, and Frank Sinatra, sponsored, fails in his second series attempt. Dinah Shore's good-night "Mmm-wah" and Pat Boone's white-buck shoes trademark two new entries, and Dick Clark's *American Bandstand* rocks coast-to-coast. . . . A young Marine colonel, John Glenn, wins $12,000 on *Name That Tune*. . . . Ernie Kovacs presents a half-hour comedy special with no dialogue. . . . The industry buzzes with talk of subliminal commercials, but the messages reaching 39 million TV homes are plain to see. There's a toothpaste that "cleans your breath while it cleans your teeth" and a hair dye that poses the question "Does she or doesn't she?"

Jack Paar: He wears his heart—and his ego—on his sleeve, and there are few personal feelings he doesn't reveal to his audience. And he's a good audience himself, encouraging verbal fireworks from guests like Alexander King (top) and Cliff Arquette.

Maverick: It adds humor to the Western formula. James Garner (pictured) plays the sardonic, untrustworthy Bret Maverick; Jack Kelly is his brother Bart.

Have Gun, Will Travel: Richard Boone is Paladin, a gunslinger with a taste for good literature and fine wine.

Wagon Train: Ward Bond (right) is the wagonmaster and Robert Horton is his scout in this high-budgeted saga of the trek westward. The series will roll on for years, with John McIntire joining the cast after Bond's death in 1961.

Zorro: Guy Williams (shown here with Myrna Fahey) is the masked avenger.

147

Perry Mason: He never loses a case. Raymond Burr is Perry and Barbara Hale is Della Street, his girl Friday, in these stories based on the Erle Stanley Gardner novels.

Richard Diamond, Private Detective: David Janssen is hunting fugitives this year; he'll be hunted himself (in a more successful series) as *The Fugitive* in 1963.

M Squad: Lee Marvin is a tough detective in this police series.

149

Leave It to Beaver: A family comedy with more charm (and better writing) than most, it stars Jerry Mathers (left) as Beaver, Tony Dow as his brother Wally. The parents are played by Hugh Beaumont and Barbara Billingsley.

Bachelor Father: Sitcom writers seem to find lots of plot possibilities in stories about mateless parents. In this one, John Forsythe is the papa; Noreen Corcoran is his niece.

150

The Real McCoys:
Hillbilly humor, with
Walter Brennan star-
ring as Grandpa Mc-
Coy; Kathy Nolan
and Richard Crenna
have supporting
roles.

The Thin Man: It's
another detective se-
ries, but this one is
laced with witty dia-
logue. Peter Lawford
and Phyllis Kirk es-
say the roles which
had endeared Wil-
liam Powell and
Myrna Loy to movie
audiences.

151

The Green Pastures: William Warfield is De Lawd in this magnificent production of Marc Connelly's fantasy. It will be repeated a year later, and that's when most people will see it; the first time around, it's on opposite the Mike Todd extravaganza.

The Lark: Another superior *Hallmark* presentation is this James Costigan adaptation of a play by Lillian Hellman. Julie Harris is Joan of Arc and Boris Karloff plays Cauchon. Also in the cast are Jack Warden, Eli Wallach, Basil Rathbone and Denholm Elliott.

Mike Todd's Party: The flamboyant producer decides to cele-
brate the first anniversary of his film "Around the World in
80 Days," and he rents Madison Square Garden for his "little party." It's a mess. Although most invited celebrities
wisely stay home, some (George Jessel, V.K. Krishna Menon)
show up for this plug-ridden exercise in self-congratulation.

1957

The Great Sebastians: Alfred Lunt and Lynn Fontanne re-create their stage success in this, their first television appearance.

There Shall Be No Night: Adapted from the acclaimed Broadway drama, it boasts outstanding performances by Charles Boyer and Katharine Cornell.

The Helen Morgan Story: Polly Bergen plays the torch-singing lead in this *Playhouse 90* dramatization.

The Seven Lively Arts: It bears a striking resemblance to *Omnibus*, but this series doesn't last very long. Critic John Crosby is the host, and the opening show, written by S.J. Perelman, is titled "The Changing Ways of Love." In the cast are Piper Laurie and Dick York (pictured) along with Mike Wallace, Rip Torn and Jason Robards Jr.

155

Pat Boone: The clean-cut young balladeer leaves the Arthur Godfrey menage for his own show this year. Boone (left) is shown here with his father-in-law, country singer Red Foley.

The Singin' Idol: Tommy Sands plays the Presley-like hero of this *Kraft* play.

American Bandstand: The rock-'n'-roll frenzy is mounting, and it carries a young Philadelphia disc jockey named Dick Clark into national prominence. His dance party graduates to the network in 1957.

Dinah Shore: She has had a 15-minute show, has made innumerable guest appearances, and has starred in specials; this year she gets an hour-long weekly series. It's a winner from the start, highlighted by the verve and imagination of its production numbers and Miss Shore's cheerful personality.

The Pied Piper of Hamelin: A musical version of the children's fable, with Van Johnson as the piper.

158

Nat King Cole: While there's no question about his talent or popularity, his show fails to attract a sponsor because, it is said, advertisers fear any association with a black entertainer.

Cinderella: Julie Andrews is the star of this 90-minute musical, written for television by Oscar Hammerstein II (left) and Richard Rodgers. Other cast members are Edie Adams, Kaye Ballard, Ilka Chase, Howard Lindsay, Alice Ghostley.

The Mike Wallace Interview: It began as a local show in New York, and now it goes coast-to-coast. Wallace browbeats the celebrity guests with tough, personal questions, but most of them are exhibitionistic (or masochistic) enough not to seem to mind.

Micronite filter.
Mild, smooth taste.
For all the right reasons.
Kent.

America's quality cigarette.
King Size or Deluxe 100's.

Micronite filter.
Mild, smooth taste.
For all the right reasons.
Kent.

Regular or Menthol.

Kings: 17 mg. "tar,"
1.1 mg. nicotine;
100's: 19 mg. "tar,"
1.3 mg. nicotine;
Menthol: 19 mg. "tar,"
1.3 mg. nicotine
av. per cigarette,
FTC Report Aug. '72.

Nikita Khrushchev: During his visit to the United States, he pauses for this interview on *Face the Nation*.

Conquest: Monkeys are used to show some aspects of "mother love" on this installment of the distinguished CBS science series.

1958
THE YEAR OF THE SCANDAL

The world of the big-money quiz ends with a bang (and considerable whimpering). Former contestants on *Dotto* and *Twenty-One* confess that the shows were rigged, 10 people are indicted for perjury, and the Big Quiz Scandal becomes the subject of daily headlines. After three years of giant ratings and overnight hero-making, it all collapses into a wallow of alibis, recriminations and double-talk. And television is left with an unsightly scar. . . . But there are brighter moments in 1958. Fred Astaire, ageless and peerless, brings his incredible artistry to TV in the first of a series of dazzling specials. Ed Sullivan devotes an entire show to the breathtaking Moiseyev Dancers. Leonard Bernstein begins his *Young People's Concerts*. Ed Murrow introduces trans-oceanic conversation with *Small World*. . . . Drama connoisseurs have much to cheer about: JP Miller's "The Days of Wine and Roses," a grim tale of alcoholic lovers; Mickey Rooney in "Eddie," a one-character tour de force; James Costigan's "Little Moon of Alban," a story of "the troubles" in Ireland; adaptations of "The Great Gatsby," "The Bridge of San Luis Rey," "Wonderful Town" and "Kiss Me, Kate." . . . For the younger set there is *Shirley Temple's Storybook,* Tab Hunter in "Hans Brinker," Sal Mineo in "Aladdin." . . . On the action scene, Lloyd Bridges is immersed in *Sea Hunt*, and the background music of Henry Mancini embroiders the suave derring-do of *Peter Gunn*. Mark Hellinger's eight million stories receive excellent treatment in the TV version of *Naked City*, and ABC's search for a young adult audience results in *77 Sunset Strip*. . . . New Good Guys on the TV range: Gene Barry twirls a cane as *Bat Masterson,* Chuck Connors twirls a .44-40 carbine as *The Rifleman*, Jock Mahoney packs a pistol in his hat as *Yancey Derringer*. . . . Garry Moore begins a prime-time variety show. . . . Tape begins to replace film. . . . Signposts of the declining importance of drama: *Kraft Theatre* dies and *Studio One* moves to Hollywood. . . . A bald giant named Mr. Clean demonstrates the fine art of kitchen swabbing, and a ubiquitous child keeps shouting, "Look, Ma! No cavities!"

Quiz Scandal: Some of those involved will say that a little cheating was necessary "to enhance the entertainment value" of the programs. But a bitterly resentful public isn't buying lame excuses, and television's image will never be the same again. Pictured here, on *Twenty-One,* are three of the people who figure prominently in the rigging investigations. Jack Barry asks the questions; in the "isolation booths" are contestants Vivienne Nearing and Charles Van Doren.

Fred Astaire: He's persuaded to try a TV special, and he brings along a new dancing partner named Barrie Chase. The old magic is still there, and the rousing success of ''An Evening with Fred Astaire'' will lead to future specials.

Kiss Me, Kate: The co-stars of the original Broadway production, Alfred Drake and Patricia Morison, repeat the hit musical on *Hallmark.*

Wonderful Town: Rosalind Russell heads the cast in the TV version of the musical.

Moiseyev Dancers: Ed Sullivan introduces this Russian folk troupe; their pyrotechnics are a 1958 standout.

Merv Griffin: The talk-show days still lie ahead when ex-vocalist Griffin emcees *Play Your Hunch*, a 1958 quizzer.

Garry Moore: After laboring for years in the unglamorous daylight hours, crew-cut Garry is finally awarded a nighttime variety hour, and it will be a consistent ratings winner for years to come. Program regulars are Marion Lorne (pictured) and Durward Kirby; later this series will showcase comedienne Carol Burnett.

Peter Gunn: Craig Stevens is the suave detective hero. Lola Albright (pictured) is his girl friend, and Herschel Bernardi plays a police lieutenant.

Naked City: Mark Hellinger's film showed the seamy underside of New York City, and this television version does the same. When the series begins in 1958 the stars are James Franciscus and John McIntire, but in 1960 the trio shown here will take over. They are (l.-r.) Horace McMahon, Paul Burke and Harry Bellaver.

169

Wanted—Dead or Alive: Not otherwise exceptional, this Western introduces future screen idol Steve McQueen.

The Rifleman: The hero is a widower raising a son, and he's quick with a carbine instead of the traditional six-shooter. Former ballplayer Chuck Connors is Lucas McCain; Johnny Crawford is his son.

170

Bat Masterson: Another gimmick Western, this one has Gene Barry (shown here with Bethel Leslie) as the foppish lead.

77 Sunset Strip: The adventures of two private eyes and a parking-lot attendant—a dubious premise, but the show becomes popular, mainly because teenies adore the car jockey, Edd "Kookie" Byrnes, who constantly riffles a comb through his hair. The gumshoes (not pictured) are Roger Smith and Efrem Zimbalist Jr.; in the episode shown here are (l.-r.) Chad Everett, Dawn Wells and Edd Byrnes.

Sea Hunt: It's a syndicated saga of the briny deep, with Lloyd Bridges as a troubleshooting skin diver.

171

Eddie: Mickey Rooney delivers a brilliant performance as a tapped-out drifter trying to raise cash.

Little Moon of Alban: James Costigan's *Hallmark* original about the Irish Rebellion of 1916 stars George Peppard and Julie Harris (pictured), Christopher Plummer and Barry Jones.

The Days of Wine and Roses: JP Miller's powerful *Playhouse 90* drama stars Piper Laurie (shown here with Charles Bickford) and Cliff Robertson as alcoholics trying to salvage their marriage and their lives.

The Winslow Boy: A drama special about an English school-boy accused of theft, it stars (l.-r.) Fredric March, Rex Thompson and Florence Eldredge.

Hansel and Gretel: The old fairy tale, with Red Buttons as Hansel.

1958

Shirley Temple's Storybook: The lovable screen moppet of the 1930's offers damatized juvenile fiction. Here, she appears with Jules Munshin in "The Legend of Sleepy Hollow."

Harvey: Mary Ellen Chase's whimsical Broadway hit will have numerous TV exposures; in this one, Art Carney stars as the amiable Elwood P. Dowd.

175

Pantomime Quiz: This game show keeps popping up through the years, usually as a summer replacement. It materializes in 1958 with (l.-r.) Howard Morris, host Mike Stokey, Carol Burnett and Milt Kamen.

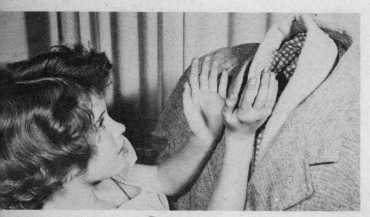

The Invisible Man: The title of this series tells the story. Here, Deborah Watling talks with her unseen uncle.

The Donna Reed Show:
In the untroubled world
of sitcom families, this
one out-wholesomes
the field. Shown here,
in an episode dealing
with an invitation to
the Varsity Prom, are
(l.-r.) Jimmy Hawkins,
Donna Reed and Shel-
ley Fabares.

Small World: Edward R.
Murrow anchors these
taped globe-spanning
conversations. In one
segment, Lauren Bacall
is one of the conferees.

177

1959
THE YEAR OF THE GANGSTER

The Untouchables arrives, awash in a sea of hijacked booze and spilled blood. It's the violent saga of syndicate crime in the Prohibition Era, and it shoots (literally) right to the top of the ratings. Dauntless crimebuster Eliot Ness is played by Robert Stack, and Neville Brand is frequently seen as Scarface Al Capone. . . . Still trying to attract a young audience to its action melodramas, ABC searches out some exotic locales. There's *Hawaiian Eye* (Connie Stevens), *Adventures in Paradise* (Gardner McKay) and *The Alaskans* (Roger Moore). . . . Jack Webb tries a new series, *Pete Kelly's Blues,* but it sounds a sour note. Screen idol Robert Taylor is more successful in *The Detectives* (one of the cops is played by Adam West, who will one day become Batman). . . . 1959 is also distinguished by the debut of *the* television Western, *Bonanza.* It's a mixture of action, soap opera and sociology, and though it gets off to a slow start, its run will eventually span three decades. Lorne Greene plays patriarch Ben Cartwright, and his sons are Michael Landon, Pernell Roberts and Dan Blocker. (Roberts' resignation in 1965 and Blocker's death in 1972 will occasion changes in cast and story emphasis.) . . . Though this is the year *Playhouse 90* is curtailed, there are some outstanding drama specials: "The Turn of the Screw" (Ingrid Bergman), "The Wicked Scheme of Jebal Deeks" (Alec Guinness), "The Moon and Sixpence" (Laurence Olivier). "People Kill People Sometimes" doesn't live up to its preshow publicity, but "What Makes Sammy Run?" (Larry Blyden) does. Lee J. Cobb stars in "I, Don Quixote," which will later be transformed into the stage hit "Man of La Mancha." . . . Ectoplasm lovers greet Rod Serling's *The Twilight Zone,* and knowledge seekers delight in *GE College Bowl.* . . . Big moments: Harry Belafonte's "Tonight with Belafonte," Menotti's operetta "The Medium," Fidel Castro's appearance on *Meet the Press.* . . . There's something for all age groups in *Dennis the Menace, The Many Loves of Dobie Gillis* and *Henessey.* . . . *See It Now* is canceled in 1959, and we are left to ponder the possibility that "Everything's better with Blue Bonnet on it."

The Untouchables: Robert Stack (left) and Jerry Paris are Federal agents in pursuit of the Chicago mob. The show first surfaces as a two-parter on *Desilu Playhouse;* it becomes a full-fledged series in 1959. Large helpings of violent action and Roaring Twenties props help make the program irresistible to viewers. Though the action takes place in the days before Mafia becomes a household word, the show will later be protested because so many of the baddies have Italian surnames.

179

Adventures in Paradise: Melodrama in the South Seas, in a series created by novelist James Michener. Aboard the yacht Tiki ("No Tiki, no watchee," one critic will write) are Gardner McKay (left) and Guy Stockwell.

Hawaiian Eye: Troy Donahue and Connie Stevens race around the pineapple fields in this detective series.

180

Staccato: When this series was first contemplated, the hero was supposed to be an adventurous jazz pianist, but this fanciful notion is discarded, and star John Cassavetes winds up playing a private eye.

Tightrope!: More cops and robbers, with Mike Connors (right, with Edward Nelson and Ann McCrea) as an undercover agent.

181

सांगत्ये ऐका

Bonanza: One of the hardiest Westerns of them all (only *Gunsmoke*, a 1955 starter, has the edge in longevity), this one chronicles life among the Cartwrights on the Ponderosa Ranch. In the original cast are (l.-r.) Michael Landon, Dan Blocker, Pernell Roberts and Lorne Greene.

CBS Reports: Current problems are scrutinized via the documentary approach. This one, filmed in India, is "The Population Explosion."

Tonight with Belafonte: Already a concert and recording star, folk singer Harry Belafonte appears in his first TV special.

At the Movies: In a special spoofing Hollywood, movie extra Sid Caesar (left) is about to be discovered by producer Art Carney, as vamp Audrey Meadows looks on.

What Makes Sammy Run?: Budd Schulberg's story is done as a two-parter on *Sunday Showcase*. Larry Blyden (center, with Monique Van Vooren) is the chiseling Sammy Glick. John Forsythe and Barbara Rush have featured roles.

The Moon and Sixpence: Robert Mulligan directs this S. Lee Pogostin adaptation of the Somerset Maugham novel. The stars are Laurence Olivier and Jessica Tandy, and they're supported by (not shown) Hume Cronyn, Judith Anderson and Geraldine Fitzgerald.

I, Don Quixote: Lee J. Cobb plays the errant knight. Dale Wasserman's script for this special will eventually become the basis for the Broadway musical "Man of La Mancha."

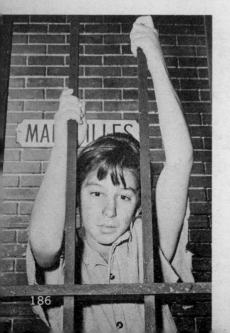

Child of Our Time: Bobby Crawford plays a Spanish refugee child in this touching Irving Gaynor Neiman teleplay for *Playhouse 90*.

186

The Twilight Zone: Ed Wynn (right) acts in "One for the Angels," one of Rod Serling's eerie tales of other worlds.

Ah, Wilderness!: The Eugene O'Neill play gets a *Hallmark* airing with (l.-r.) Burgess Meredith, Lee Kinsolving, Helen Hayes and Lloyd Nolan.

187

1960
THE YEAR OF THE GREAT DEBATES

John F. Kennedy and Richard M. Nixon, the Presidential candidates in this election year, appear in four television debates. In the first confrontation (they are not really debates, in the classic sense) Kennedy projects an image of youthful self-assurance; Nixon, without makeup and perspiring freely, is markedly less appealing. Most viewers judge Kennedy "the winner," and it is agreed that his campaign has gained great impetus. . . . Jack Paar, miffed when network censors delete a dubious joke, walks out on his show in January, goes to Hong Kong, and is persuaded to return in March. . . . No longer Mr. Television, Milton Berle becomes host of something called *Jackpot Bowling*. . . . Lucille Ball and Desi Arnaz split up. . . . CBS presents a hard-hitting (and controversial) documentary on migrant farm workers, "Harvest of Shame." . . . Maurice Chevalier does his first special, Sinatra and Presley team up for another, and Leland Hayward produces a two-hour extravaganza, "The Fabulous Fifties." . . . On the other hand, NBC makes a special out of a dreadful movie, "Rivak the Barbarian." . . . Some notable performances in 1960: Art Carney in "Harvey," Judith Anderson in "The Cradle Song," Martin Balsam and Arthur Hill in Reginald Rose's two-parter "The Sacco-Vanzetti Story." . . . Andy Griffith starts his enormously popular situation comedy; Fred MacMurray hits paydirt with another one-parent comedy, *My Three Sons*. . . . Primitive characters and some prehistoric jokes are featured in an animated-cartoon series, *The Flintstones*. . . . Martin Milner, George Maharis and a white convertible are the stars of *Route 66*. Other crime-and-punishment sagas: *Checkmate* (Anthony George, Doug McClure and Sebastian Cabot as private eyes), *Hong Kong* (Rod Taylor), *Thriller* (narrated by Boris Karloff) and *SurfSide 6* (Troy Donahue). . . . Lest we wander too far into the world of fantasy, the commercials bring us back to reality. We are told about "coffee-er coffee." We see a cloth ravaged by concentrated stomach acid. And we are asked: "What's the amazing new way to drain your nasal sinus area?"

The Great Debates: Television plays a central role in the 1960 Presidential campaign, although no one will ever be certain just how much these "debates" influence the election. Candidate Nixon (right), generally adjudged second best in these meetings, learns some valuable lessons about TV makeup and lighting.

Macbeth: The Thane gets his second *Hallmark* outing, this one starring Judith Anderson and, again, Maurice Evans.

The Sacco-Vanzetti Story: This Reginald Rose teleplay, a two-parter, is an example of the "documentary dramas" which emerge briefly as more conventional drama begins to fade from view. The Golden Age is ending. Here, during rehearsal, are (l.-r.) Martin Balsam as Nicola Sacco, E. G. Marshall as attorney William Thompson and Arthur Hill as Bartolomeo Vanzetti.

The Iceman Cometh: This four-hour version of the O'Neill play, starring Jason Robards Jr., is shown on educational stations via David Susskind's *The Play of the Week*.

Checkmate: About a trio of private eyes, it stars Sebastian Cabot (left, with Carolyn Craig and Dana Andrews). The other two sleuths are played by Doug McClure and Anthony George.

Route 66: A couple of adventurers tour the country (in an auto produced by the show's sponsor). Here, stars George Maharis (left) and Martin Milner are joined by guest Inger Stevens.

SurfSide 6: More private eyes, this time based on a Florida houseboat. In the cast are (l.-r.) Lee Patterson, Troy Donahue, Diane McBain and Van Williams.

The Roaring Twenties: Dorothy Provine is Pinky Pinkham, star entertainer at The Charleston Club, in this action series.

193

My Three Sons: And still another motherless brood, this one shepherded by Fred MacMurray (shown here with his youngest "son," Stanley Livingston). The other siblings are Tim Considine and Don Grady; William Frawley is the grandfather.

194

The Andy Griffith Show: He came to prominence with a hit comedy record, and in this first TV effort he plays the sheriff of a small town called Mayberry. Griffith (left) is shown here with guest Sterling Holloway.

1961
THE YEAR OF THE SURLY SURGEON

The Surly Surgeon is *Ben Casey*, destined to scowl his way into Nielsen's Top 10, along with another new medical man, *Dr. Kildare*. Lawyers are represented in 1961 too—*The Defenders* arrives and soon becomes TV's most respected (if not most watched) weekly series. . . . There are lots of prosperous newcomers—*The Dick Van Dyke Show* (though it almost gets canceled before finding its audience), *Hazel, Mister Ed, Sing Along with Mitch, Walt Disney's Wonderful World of Color* (swiped by NBC from ABC), *Saturday Night at the Movies* (the start of a prime-time movie trend), *The Steve Allen Show*. But many more last only briefly—*Window on Main Street* (Robert Young), *Mrs. G Goes to College* (Gertrude Berg), new Ernie Kovacs and Bob Cummings shows, *Top Cat, Alvin and the Chipmunks, The Hathaways, Ichabod and Me, Father of the Bride, The Bob Newhart Show* (which wins an Emmy after being canceled), *87th Precinct, Cain's Hundred, Frontier Circus, Follow the Sun, Acapulco, Malibu Run*, etc. . . . Shortest lived of all is *You're in the Picture*, a Jackie Gleason game show that is so terrible Gleason abandons it and spends the second week apologizing to the audience. . . . John Kennedy is inaugurated. Presidential news conferences are telecast live for the first time. . . . Alan Shepard and Virgil Grissom take America's first trips into space. . . . Edward R. Murrow quits TV to head up the USIA. *David Brinkley's Journal* is on weekly. John Chancellor succeeds Dave Garroway on *Today*. . . . Biggest drama specials, in a year containing very few non-series dramas: "The Power and the Glory" (Laurence Olivier, Julie Harris, George C. Scott) and "Victoria Regina" (Julie Harris). . . . Other notable specials: "The Real West" (Gary Cooper), "A Self-Portrait: Vincent Van Gogh" (Lee J. Cobb) and "The Gershwin Years." . . . The FCC's new chairman, Newton Minow, tells the TV industry that its programming is "a vast wasteland." The Senate, investigating TV violence, singles out episodes of *Bus Stop* ("A Lion Walks Among Us," with Fabian) and *Whispering Smith* (starring Audie Murphy) as particularly reprehensible examples. . . . Italian-Americans boycott *The Untouchables*. . . . Stan Freberg has America laughing about chow mein; Katie Winters has it worrying about body odor.

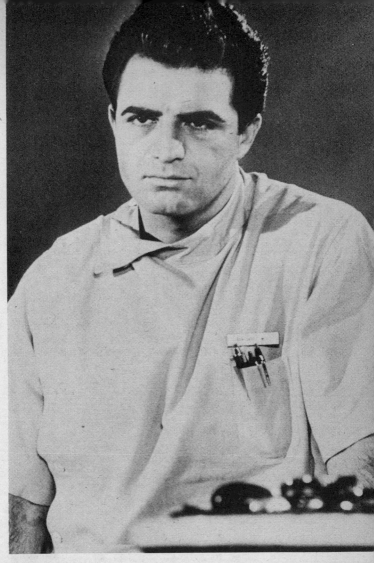

Ben Casey: Vincent Edwards stars as Casey, the headstrong chief resident in neurosurgery at County General Hospital. Sam Jaffe is cast as his mentor, Dr. Zorba.

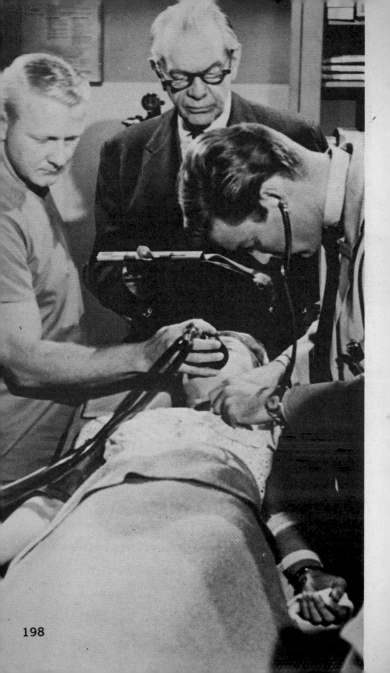

The Defenders: The protagonists are a pair of lawyers—
Lawrence Preston (E. G. Marshall) and his son Kenneth
(Robert Reed). Although its action remains within the traditional confines of courtroom drama, *The Defenders* attempts
to get its viewers thinking about moral questions while they
worry whether the Prestons will be able to prove their clients'
innocence. During its four years on TV, the series will win
many prizes for scripts and acting.

Dr. Kildare: Drama series of this era typically pair a young
hero with an older one. In this one, based on MGM movies,
young Dr. Kildare of Blair General Hospital is played by
Richard Chamberlain (with stethoscope), and old Dr. Gilles-
pie by Raymond Massey (holding clipboard).   199

The Dick Van Dyke Show: The early ratings are weak, but this comedy series will ultimately become a TV classic. The stars (pictured) are Dick Van Dyke and Mary Tyler Moore, with Morey Amsterdam, Rose Marie and Richard Deacon leading the supporting cast. Carl Reiner is in charge of the scripts, which for several seasons will set the standards for comedy writing in television.

Hazel: Shirley Booth plays an unpredictable maid in this long-running series based on Ted Key's cartoons in the Saturday Evening Post.

1961

The Hathaways: One season is all viewers can take of this series about a family (led by Peggy Cass) and its chimpanzees (the Marquis Chimps). Pictured: Jacqueline Detroy with Candy.

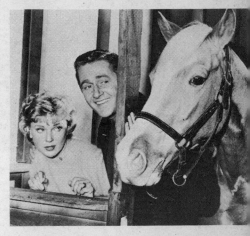

Mister Ed: He's a talking horse, and he'll probably last forever, in reruns. His straight men are Alan Young and Connie Hines.

Car 54, Where Are You?: Joe E. Ross (left) and Fred Gwynne are a pair of bird-brained cops—Toody and Muldoon—in this Nat Hiken series.

201

Inauguration: As President Kennedy's inauguration is telecast, viewers do not know that they are looking at four once and future Presidents—behind Kennedy stand Lyndon Johnson and Richard Nixon; behind Chief Justice Earl Warren (administering the oath) is Dwight Eisenhower. Also in the picture are Jacqueline Kennedy (far left), and Adlai Stevenson and Dean Rusk (above Eisenhower).

The Real West: Shortly before his death Gary Cooper narrates this *Project 20* documentary, which punctures myths about the Old West.

1961

Space Shot: The U.S. moves a small step closer to the moon, as its first astronaut, Alan Shepard, is launched into space, briefly, and returned safely to earth. Here, TV newsman Jules Bergman interviews him.

203

Bus Stop: This series achieves unwelcome notoriety when one of its episodes (starring Fabian and based on a novel by Tom Wicker) is condemned for its violence by critics and congressmen. Here, in a milder episode, are (l.-r.) Marilyn Maxwell, Tuesday Weld and Gary Lockwood.

The Law and Mr. Jones: James Whitmore stars as a high-principled attorney in this comedy-drama series that is canceled after a few months, despite many viewers' protests.

Sing Along with Mitch: The beat is bouncy and the songs familiar. Mitch Miller's *Sing Along* specials prove so popular, NBC gives the ebullient maestro a weekly series in the fall of 1961.

Who Do You Trust?: In 1961 Johnny Carson (with Reggie Dombeck here) is trying to attract attention as host of this daytime quiz show (he succeeded Edgar Bergen).

205

1962
THE YEAR OF THE HILLBILLIES

The Beverly Hillbillies clomps into television, giving CBS a new hit show, beginning a rural-comedy trend and providing a convenient target for those who believe that TV entertainment has finally sunk as low as it can go. Little do they know. . . . The most dramatic, suspenseful programs of the year star *real* people and events—the Cuban missile crisis and the first astronauts to orbit the earth (John Glenn, Scott Carpenter and Wally Schirra). This is the year, too, during which Richard Nixon tells the press that it won't have him "to kick around any more." . . . Johnny Carson takes over *The Tonight Show*, succeeding Jack Paar, who becomes one of several TV veterans returning in new—and mostly unsuccessful—series. Paar's is a weekly variety hour; Jackie Gleason's is his *American Scene Magazine;* Loretta Young's is a drama half-hour; Groucho Marx's is *Tell It to Groucho;* Andy Williams' is a variety hour; and Sid Caesar's is nine specials called *As Caesar Sees It.* . . . Among the other 1962 series are the first 90-minute Western—*The Virginian;* a barrage of war dramas and comedies—*Combat, The Gallant Men, McHale's Navy, Ensign O'Toole;* and such other items as *Sam Benedict, The Nurses, The Jetsons, Stoney Burke, Empire, Oh, Those Bells!* and *Going My Way* (with Gene Kelly). . . . Major entertainment specials: "Julie and Carol at Carnegie Hall," "Cyrano" (with Christopher Plummer this time) and "Noah and the Flood" (a Balanchine-Stravinsky misfire). . . . The networks are on the defensive. "Biography of a Bookie Joint" and "The Battle of Newburgh" provoke protests—and win prizes for journalistic enterprise. The Senate is investigating TV violence, and Hollywood cuts down on the bloodshed—until ratings begin to suffer. And Howard K. Smith is condemned for inviting Alger Hiss to tell TV viewers what he thinks of Richard Nixon. . . . Telstar, the first communications satellite, is launched. . . . Hertz is dropping people into driver's seats, the Li'l Old Winemaker is busy with his grapes, and the FCC orders Rapid Shave to quit claiming that it can perform miracles with sandpaper.

The Beverly Hillbillies: Irene Ryan (pictured) is Granny Clampett; Buddy Ebsen, Jed Clampett; and Donna Douglas and Max Baer Jr., their children. The producer-writer is Paul Henning, and this is the first of several rustic comedy hits (*Petticoat Junction, Green Acres*) for him.

I'm Dickens . . . He's Fenster: And they're both klutzes—a pair of inept handymen, played by Marty Ingels (pictured) and John Astin.

It's a Man's World: It's the story of some kids living on a houseboat, told in quiet, leisurely fashion. Too quiet and leisurely for most viewers—the show is canceled, though its admirers protest vigorously. The cast: Ted Bessell (pictured), Glenn Corbett, Randy Boone, Jan Norris, Mike Burns.

McHale's Navy: From Bilko to *M*A*S*H*, military comedy is a TV staple. This time a PT-boat squadron is the setting, and the stars are Ernest Borgnine, Joe Flynn (pictured) and Tim Conway.

The Virginian: The difference between this TV Western and others is its length—90 minutes. James Drury plays the title role, supported by Lee J. Cobb (pictured), Doug McClure and numerous later additions to the cast.

Julie and Carol at Carnegie Hall: Carol Burnett (left) and Julie Andrews team up for the year's biggest entertainment special, produced by Bob Banner and written by Mike Nichols and Ken Welch.

Johnny Carson: He takes over *The Tonight Show* from Jack Paar in 1962, bringing announcer Ed McMahon and orchestra leader Skitch Henderson with him. He soon establishes himself as a late-night fixture, consistently outrating — and outlasting — whatever the other networks throw at him, year after year, into the 1970's.

Andy Williams: After years as a perennial summer replacement, he gets his own regular-season series in 1962 and manages to survive the vagaries of American musical tastes longer than most TV singers. In this show, in the late 1960's, he spoofs a Wagnerian opera with Jo Anne Worley.

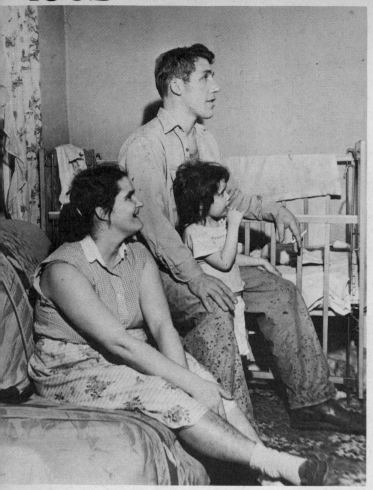

The Battle of Newburgh: This controversial *NBC White Paper* exposes the plight of poor families (like this one) in Newburgh, N.Y., where welfare payments have been cut off.

Cuban Missile Crisis: It erupts in October, and part of the tense international drama is played out on television. Here, UN Ambassador Adlai Stevenson relentlessly challenges the Soviet delegate, Valerian Zorin, to deny that there are Russian missiles in Cuba.

The Tunnel: It shows the escape of 59 East Berliners to the West. The program is delayed by a nervous State Department but finally reaches the air in December, narrated by Piers Anderton (shown here at the West Berlin end of the escape tunnel).

1963
THE YEAR OF THE ASSASSIN

They call it "the week television came of age." It is a harrowing week for the American people. But for television it is a time for rising to a dreadful occasion—the murder of a President. In the aftermath comes another killing, as the accused assassin is himself assassinated—in plain sight of millions of television viewers. Everyone who sits through those awful days in November knows that this is one television experience he will never be able to forget. . . . There are now 50 million TV homes, and among other things being watched in them are a massively impressive civil-rights "March on Washington" (Martin Luther King: "I have a dream") and the first live pictures from space (Gordon Cooper orbits the earth). . . . Women are busy. Ingrid Bergman plays "Hedda Gabler"; Julie Harris does "Pygmalion"; Princess Grace tours Monaco; and Elizabeth Taylor, London. A cheerful, uninhibited woman named Julia Child presents a special called "The French Chef" that will soon be converted into Educational TV's first hit series. . . . 1963 has its programming disasters too. A grandiose two-hour weekly Jerry Lewis series is a spectacular failure. Judy Garland's series is trampled by *Bonanza*. *100 Grand* flops in its attempt to revive big-money quizzes. *Arrest and Trial* is more trying than arresting as the first—and last—tandem of 45-minute dramas. *The New Phil Silvers Show* (he's a factory foreman) doesn't match the old one. Imogene Coca strikes out as a maid (*Grindl*), George C. Scott as a social worker (*East Side/West Side*), Richard Boone as leader of a TV repertory company, and Keefe Brasselle as star of *The Keefe Brasselle Show*. . . . Some newcomers do better—*The Fugitive, Petticoat Junction, Burke's Law, My Favorite Martian, The Farmer's Daughter, Monday Night at the Movies*. . . . Instant replay is used for the first time. . . . Walter Cronkite takes over CBS's evening news, competing with Huntley and Brinkley, and both shows expand to 30 minutes. Hugh Downs replaces John Chancellor as *Today* host. . . . ABC doesn't think the nation should listen to Pete Seeger and The Weavers (they're "controversial") and refuses to let them sing on *Hootenanny*. . . . Meanwhile, America is learning all about "greasy kid stuff."

Assassination and Funeral: Mrs. John F. Kennedy and her children, Caroline and John Jr., wait to be driven to the Capitol rotunda, where the body of the murdered President lies in state. In Dallas, at almost the same moment, Lee Harvey Oswald is shot by Jack Ruby, as America watches on its television sets.

Mr. Novak: He's an English teacher at Jefferson High, played by James Franciscus (left), with Dean Jagger as the principal.

East Side/West Side: This series about a social worker comes up with some good scripts and performances but fails to attract a mass audience. George C. Scott (here with Diana van der Vlis) stars as Neil Brock. The cast also includes Elizabeth Wilson and Cicely Tyson.

216

The Fugitive: Dr. Richard Kimble (David Janssen, seated) keeps running, week after week, evading the implacable Inspector Gerard (Barry Morse) and seeking the one-armed man who killed his wife. Here, he takes refuge in an Indian school (with Hope Lange and Jaime Sanchez).

217

Judy Garland: She starts a weekly series in the fall of 1963 with high hopes—and personal frailties, production problems and network tampering. When spring arrives, Judy is gone, victimized by her own show's failures and the overpowering ratings of its competition, *Bonanza*. In one show, Garland (right) sings with two generations of belters—Barbra Streisand (left) and Ethel Merman.

Danny Kaye: He fares better than Garland. His series, with broader appeal and a better time slot, lasts for several seasons. In this production number, Kaye dances with Gwen Verdon.

Julia Child: *The French Chef* has no songs or dances— just Julia Child making the preparation of gourmet dishes a treat.

Let's Make a Deal: Covetous contestants in crazy costumes gamble for big prizes, while Monty Hall eggs them on. It proves to be a winning— and long-running— formula.

219

1964
THE YEAR OF THE GREAT ESCAPISM

Americans seem to be yearning for escape in 1964, and television provides a number of eccentric ways for viewers to get away from it all. There is a phenomenon called *The Man from U.N.C.L.E.*; a headlong plunge into the bizarre, with *The Munsters, The Addams Family, My Living Doll* and *Bewitched;* a nighttime soap opera, *Peyton Place;* a new series called *Gilligan's Island*, which achieves recognition as the most idiotic program ever—undeserved, perhaps, considering the fact that in this season alone it is accompanied by such worthy competitors as *The Baileys of Balboa, Wendy and Me, Broadside, 90 Bristol Court, Many Happy Returns, Mickey, Valentine's Day, The Tycoon* and *Gomer Pyle, U.S.A.* . . . Still, there are some respectable programming innovations to point to: *That Was the Week That Was, Profiles in Courage, Slattery's People, Shindig*. . . . It's a really big year for Ed Sullivan—he presents The Beatles and The Singing Nun. And when he tries to give comedian Jackie Mason the hook, Mason gives him the finger—right here, on our stage. . . . On the political stage, the new star is Lyndon Johnson. Viewers watch him deliver his first State of the Union address, and go on to trounce Barry Goldwater in the November election. . . . But the public is becoming aware of something else, too. The Vietnam War is moving into their living rooms in 1964, and there is no escape from the disturbing realities that are slowly seeping into the national consciousness. . . . CBS humiliates Walter Cronkite, pulling him out of his anchor seat for the Democratic Convention and substituting Robert Trout and Roger Mudd. The desperation effort to cut into NBC's convention ratings lead is an embarrassing failure. . . . Carol Burnett hurts her neck, flops in a series called *The Entertainers* but redeems herself in a special, "Once upon a Mattress." . . . The King Family floods the screen with the first of its numberless numbing specials. . . . Syncom II, lofted into a "stationary" orbit above the equator, becomes the first working synchronous communications satellite. . . . *The Friday Night Fights* are kayoed and, for the first time, there are no weekly network boxing telecasts. . . . A White Knight and a White Tornado keep interrupting the programs. And the Doublemint Twins are exhorting people to double their fun.

The Man from U.N.C.L.E.: He's Napoleon Solo (Robert Vaughn—rear), who teams up with Illya Kuryakin (David McCallum) to outmaneuver the sinister agents from THRUSH. It's all done tongue-in-cheek, with lots of help from ultra-modern gadgets and implausible plot twists. Leo G. Carroll is U.N.C.L.E.'s head man.

The Rogues: More tongue-in-cheek adventures, with a dash of sophistication, as a clan of charming con men concocts elaborate schemes to enrich the family coffers. The Rogues are (l.-r.) Charles Boyer, Gig Young, David Niven and Robert Coote, plus Gladys Cooper.

222

Bewitched: Of the many supernatural comedies that materialize in 1964, *Bewitched* proves the most successful. It stars Elizabeth Montgomery, with Richard York (later replaced by Dick Sargent) and Agnes Moorehead.

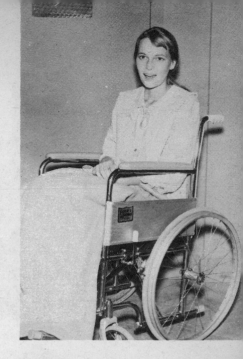

Peyton Place: Soap opera, based on Grace Metalious's gamey novel, comes to nighttime TV twice a week and launches the careers of such actors as Mia Farrow (pictured) and Ryan O'Neal. Other early members of the constantly changing cast include Dorothy Malone, Barbara Parkins, Ed Nelson and George Macready.

Mr. Broadway: The first and last attempt to make a TV hero out of a Broadway press agent is one of 1964's flops. Craig Stevens (with Barbara Feldon here) is the urbane flack.

223

1964

The Munsters: This is one of two monster families who move into TV this year (the other: *The Addams Family*) for a short stay. Fred Gwynne and Yvonne DeCarlo play Herman and Lily Munster.

Gilligan's Island: Critics hate this broadly played series, but that doesn't discourage viewers, and *Gilligan's Island* will run for years, with Bob Denver and Dawn Wells as two of the stars.

Flipper: In this children's series man's best friend is a dolphin. Flipper's human companions are Brian Kelly, Tommy Norden and Luke Halpin.

Gomer Pyle, USMC: It's a spinoff from *The Andy Griffith Show,* which is why Griffith and Ronny Howard turn up in this episode, visiting Gomer (Jim Nabors) and his drill sergeant (Frank Sutton) at boot camp.

The Beatles: Ed Sullivan scores a coup, signing up The Beatles for their first U.S. TV appearance.

Sophia Loren: In the mid-Sixties she is the subject of countless TV specials. This one is "Sophia Loren in Rome."

1964

That Was the Week That Was: Also known as *TW3*, it introduces topical satire to weekly TV, with such performers as (l.-r.) Nancy Ames, Phyllis Newman and Pat Englund, as well as David Frost (who had starred in the original British *TW3*).

The Les Crane Show: ABC decides to compete with NBC's *Tonight Show*, plunking a talk jockey named Les Crane down in the middle of a round set (here Crane chats with a wrestler). The late-night experiment lasts only a few months.

227

The Olympics: Tokyo is the scene of this summer's Games, covered comprehensively by TV, as they are every four years. Here, the Olympics begin, as a runner carries the torch into a Tokyo stadium.

The Louvre: TV cameras are allowed inside the Paris museum, to give viewers a glimpse of its treasures and an account of its history, narrated by Charles Boyer.

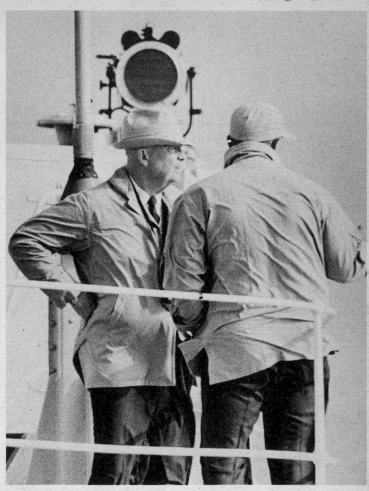

D-Day Plus 20: Dwight Eisenhower returns to Normandy, accompanied by Walter Cronkite, to relive the 1944 invasion, on *CBS Reports.*

1965
THE YEAR OF THE TALKING CAR

The far-fetched-comedy trend escalates in 1965 with, among others, *My Mother, the Car, Camp Runamuck, Hogan's Heroes, F Troop, Get Smart, Hank, Gidget, Mona McCluskey, I Dream of Jeannie, O.K. Crackerby*, and a Smothers Brothers sitcom that has Tommy playing an angel. . . . It's time for a new round of Westerns—or is it? A lot of them ride in—*The Loner, The Wild Wild West, Laredo, Branded, The Big Valley, A Man Called Shenandoah, The Legend of Jesse James*—but almost all of them are gunned down by the ratings. . . . *I Spy* proves that America is finally ready to accept a black man as star of a TV series. . . . Dean Martin moves in for a long stay as star of his own variety series. Steve Lawrence (*The Steve Lawrence Show*) and Peter Falk (*Trials of O'Brien*) are not so fortunate. . . . It's a bountiful year for specials. A young singer does her first—"My Name Is Barbra." A once-young singer does his best—"Frank Sinatra: A Man and His Music." "Cinderella" is revived, with Lesley Ann Warren in the role originated by Julie Andrews (who joins Gene Kelly in a 1965 special). Lunt and Fontanne star in "The Magnificent Yankee"; Fredric March and Ed Begley in "Inherit the Wind"; and Michelangelo in a two-hour documentary. . . . News departments cover Winston Churchill's funeral, Pope Paul's visit, Lady Bird Johnson's White House tour, Col. Edward White's "space walk," the first live pickup from a space-shoot recovery ship (Gemini VII), riots in Berkeley and Watts, the buildup of American manpower in Vietnam, and anti-Vietnam teach-ins on college campuses. . . . The first commercial satellite, Early Bird, is used for "Town Meetings of the World." Other offbeat documentaries: "The Mystery of Stonehenge," "The National Drivers' Test." . . . The father of *all* TV documentaries, Edward R. Murrow, is dead at 57. . . . Two of TV's most powerful figures, James Aubrey of CBS and Robert Kintner of NBC, are fired. . . . It's the last network year for *Perry Mason* and *The Dick Van Dyke Show*, the first for Charlie Brown. . . . *The Beatles* (a Saturday-morning cartoon series) and Walter Cronkite (finally overtaking Huntley and Brinkley) clean up in the ratings. . . . Viewers are being urged to put tigers in their tanks and join the Dodge Rebellion.

My Mother the Car: The late Mrs. Crabtree returns to haunt her son in the form of an old car (equipped with Ann Sothern's voice). Here, sitting in Mother, are (l.-r.) Randy Whipple, Maggie Pierce, Cindy Eilbacher and Jerry Van Dyke.

1965

Get Smart: Maxwell Smart is a dumb-cluck secret agent in this spoof of James Bondian superheroes. Don Adams, playing Smart (whose shoe is also a telephone), popularizes such phrases as "Sorry about that, Chief" and "Would you believe . . .?" Barbara Feldon co-stars as Agent 99, who eventually marries Smart.

Green Acres: It's the flip side of *The Beverly Hillbillies.* Eva Gabor and Eddie Albert, as a pair of sophisticates, move to the farm (and get less fan mail than their co-star Arnold the Pig).

232

I Dream of Jeannie: With Barbara Eden as a genie and Larry Hagman as her master, *Jeannie* becomes a perennially popular series.

Hogan's Heroes: A German prisoner-of-war camp is the unlikely locale of another hit comedy series. The cast includes (l.-r.) Bob Crane, Werner Klemperer and John Banner.

233

1965

Camp Runamuck: The three visible tub toters are (l.-r.) Dave Ketchum, Dave Madden and Arch Johnson, as inept counselors at a summer camp.

F Troop: 1965 is a big year for ineptitude. This pair of bunglers (Forrest Tucker and Larry Storch) does its fouling up in the U.S. Cavalry (abetted by Ken Berry).

234

Gidget: Sally Fields is the teen-age surf freak; Don Porter, her father.

Supermarket Sweep: Some observers consider this David Susskind series the ultimate game show. Badgered by their wives, contestants in gym clothes race around a store, competing to see who can load his cart with the most and costliest merchandise.

235

1965

I Spy: It's a breakthrough for black actors when Bill Cosby is cast to co-star with Robert Culp (as Alexander Scott and Kelly Robinson) in this series. The two men establish a breezy rapport that adds an appealing touch of freshness to the standard foreign-intrigue plots.

The FBI: Based—very loosely—on FBI files, the series arrives in 1965 for a long Sunday-night stay. Efrem Zimbalist Jr. (pictured) stars with William Reynolds and Philip Abbott.

Run for Your Life: Paul Bryan (Ben Gazzara) is running because doctors have told him he has only two years to live, and he wants to live them to the hilt.

Secret Agent: Patrick McGoohan plays John Drake of British Intelligence in this crisp import from Britain.

237

My Name Is Barbra:
It's the first of several TV specials for Barbra Streisand, who, at the age of 22, is the hottest thing in show business in 1965.

Frank Sinatra: A Man and His Music: There are two specials with this title. The first, in 1965, is Sinatra's most effective TV hour ever. The sequel, a year later, pairs Sinatra with his daughter Nancy (pictured).

Dean Martin: The success of his easygoing 1965 series sparks a comeback for TV variety shows, which have been in eclipse in recent seasons. Here, Martin (left) and Zero Mostel do a Shakespearean sketch.

Mike Douglas: His talk-variety show starts in Cleveland (where this picture was shot in 1965, with Craig Stevens— right—as a guest), then moves to Philadelphia in 1966. Despite its location outside of the big TV production centers and its lack of a network tie-up, *The Mike Douglas Show* outlasts many higher-powered competitors and becomes a daytime-TV institution.

Vietnam: The U.S. involvement in Vietnam is being stepped up, and so is TV coverage of the war—and of the growing opposition to it. In this documentary, "Vietnam: December, 1965," Garrick Utley, NBC's Saigon bureau chief, interviews some GI's.

Papal Visit: In 1965 Pope Paul VI pays a brief visit to America and meets with President Johnson.

1966
THE YEAR OF THE BAT

Holy Nielsens! It's *Batman*—adapted from the comic strip, with campy flavoring added. It becomes the most talked-about show of the year. . . . As 1966 progresses, it is evident that this is going to be a year of novelties: *Mission: Impossible, Star Trek, The Avengers, The Monkees, The Dating Game, The Newlywed Game, Dark Shadows*. And some others that don't work: *The Green Hornet, T.H.E. Cat, The Girl from U.N.C.L.E., Run Buddy Run, It's About Time*. . . . It's not an auspicious year for comebacks. Viewers snub Milton Berle and Garry Moore in variety hours, Ann Sheridan in *Pistols and Petticoats*, Jean Arthur in *The Jean Arthur Show* and Red Buttons in *The Secret Life of Henry Phyffe*. . . . Sammy Davis Jr., Phyllis Diller, Robert Goulet, Tammy Grimes and Burt Reynolds also go down with sinking shows. But *That Girl* and *Family Affair* settle in for long stays. . . . The smashing ratings of "The Bridge on the River Kwai" add momentum to the prime-time movie trend, which already finds the networks showing movies five nights out of seven. . . . There is talk, too, about the dawn of a new era of television drama, as "Death of a Salesman" (Lee J. Cobb) and "The Glass Menagerie" (Shirley Booth) are well-received, and *ABC Stage 67* promises a season of weekly productions, many of them dramas. . . . A man claims that he rigged the ratings of a Carol Channing special. . . . Fred Friendly, head of CBS News, resigns in protest after his network telecasts the usual daytime reruns of *I Love Lucy* instead of pre-empting them to carry Senate hearings on the escalating Vietnam War. . . . TV does cover the White House wedding of Luci Baines Johnson to Patrick Nugent. . . . Ronald Reagan gives up his role as host of *Death Valley Days*, to run for Governor of California. . . . Sen. Everett Dirksen performs on *The Hollywood Palace*. . . . Rowan and Martin are Dean Martin's summer replacement. . . . CBS is charging $70,000 a minute for commercials in the NFL championship game. . . . Two pipe dreams come together when the Overmyer Network signs a three-year contract to carry the games of the Continental Football League. . . . Nearly all prime-time programming is in color. . . . The people in commercials are saying, "You've got bad breath. *Bad breath!*" and "Mother, I'd rather do it *myself!*"

Batman: A carefully contrived, stylized put-on, it's an immediate hit, twice a week. Adam West (pictured) is appropriately stolid as Bruce Wayne, alias Batman; and Burt Ward is suitably impetuous as Dick Grayson, alias Robin the Boy Wonder.

1966

Death of a Salesman: Arthur Miller's tragedy is revived, with Lee J. Cobb (pictured) repeating his original Broadway role, supported by Mildred Dunnock and George Segal.

The Love Song of Barney Kempinski: Alan Arkin stars with Arlene Golonka in Murray Schisgal's wild comedy, which kicks off a weekly series of specials that is called *ABC Stage 67* even though it starts in the fall of '66.

The Bridge on the River Kwai: It was a blockbuster of a movie, and now the movie is a blockbuster of a TV show, sweeping the Sunday-night ratings and sending network vice presidents scurrying to find more movies for television showings.

A Christmas Memory: *ABC Stage 67*'s greatest triumph is this Truman Capote play. Geraldine Page stars with Donnie Melvin.

Mission: Impossible: After a modest start, it becomes one of the most talked-about shows ("Your mission, Mr. Phelps . . . ," "This tape will self-destruct in . . ."). The original cast: Steven Hill, Martin Landau, Barbara Bain, Greg Morris, Peter Lupus. Later, Hill, Landau and Bain will depart; Peter Graves, Leonard Nimoy, Lesley Warren, Lynda Day George and Barbara Anderson will arrive. Here, baseball's Johnny Bench (right) turns actor to appear with Graves and Warren in 1971.

Tarzan: Edgar Rice Burroughs' jungle hero swings into television in 1966, impersonated by Ron Ely (with Barbara Bouchet and Fernando Lamas here).

1966

Star Trek: The devotees of this space-adventure series are staunchly loyal —and will remain so long after the show has gone out of production. William Shatner is the starship commander, but Leonard Nimoy (pictured), as the pointy-eared Mr. Spock, gets most of the fan mail.

Hawk: Burt Reynolds (left) is Det. Lt. John Hawk, an Iroquois Indian on the New York police force. Wayne Grice plays his young assistant.

The Avengers: John Steed and Emma Peel (Patrick Macnee and Diana Rigg) deal efficiently and dispassionately with all sorts of diabolically evil schemers in one of the few British series that manages to catch on in the U.S.

24

The Monkees: Tricky visual effects and an unabashed attempt to cash in on the success of The Beatles are the principal features of this unorthodox comedy-and-music series. The Monkees are (l.-r.) Peter Tork, Mike Nesmith, Micky Dolenz and Davy Jones.

1966

That Girl: It makes a star of Marlo Thomas, daughter of Danny. Ted Bessell (with her here) plays her boy friend.

Dark Shadows: The weirdest arrival of 1966 is a gothic soap opera featuring a vampire named Barnabas (Jonathan Frid).

Family Affair: A bachelor father (Brian Keith), a bearded butler (Sebastian Cabot) and three kids (l.-r., Kathy Garver, Anissa Jones, Johnnie Whitaker) are the ingredients of this sitcom.

1967
THE YEAR OF THE SUPER BOWL

The champions of the two rival pro-football leagues are playing each other for the first time. CBS and NBC combine forces
for the Super Bowl telecast, with their sportscasters sharing
the broadcasting booth. After all the pregame hoopla, the
football contest itself is an anticlimax. The Green Bay Packers
uphold the honor of the National Football League (and CBS),
convincingly beating the Kansas City Chiefs of the American
Football League, 35-10. . . . ABC devotes an entire night's
schedule to a study of Africa. CBS News telecasts "The Anderson Platoon," "The Italians" (Luigi Barzini) and a conversation with Eric Hoffer. . . . Dramas: "Do Not Go Gentle into
That Good Night" (Melvyn Douglas), "The Final War of
Ollie Winter" (Ivan Dixon), "Mark Twain Tonight" (Hal
Holbrook), "The Crucible" (George C. Scott). . . . Other
specials: "Annie Get Your Gun" (Ethel Merman), "Damn
Yankees" and hours with Zero Mostel, Lena Horne, Debbie
Reynolds, Jack Paar, Frank Sinatra, Flanders and Swann,
James Bond and Twiggy. A sleeper special called "Laugh-In"
is so well received, NBC plans to turn it into a weekly series.
. . . Johnny Carson says he's "sick" and the only thing that
will cure him is a pay raise. NBC makes him well, and he returns to *The Tonight Show*. Carson has some new late-night
competition—Joey Bishop on ABC. . . . An AFTRA strike
turns Arnold Zenker into a TV star—for a week. . . . *The
Fugitive* stops running on network TV, and a waiting world
learns who killed Helen Kimble. . . . Movies are on six nights
a week now. "Never on Sunday" fills one of them, proving that
some censorship barriers are falling. . . . Educational TV goes
"Public" with the launching of a full national network and an
ambitious but erratic Sunday-night series called *PBL*. . . . Also
new in 1967: *The Smothers Brothers Comedy Hour, The
Carol Burnett Show, Ironside, Mannix, Judd for the Defense,
He and She, The Flying Nun, Captain Nice, Mr. Terrific, The
Invaders, Gentle Ben, Cimarron Strip, Hondo, Custer, Cowboy
in Africa, The High Chaparral*, and short-lived variety ventures starring Danny Thomas, Steve Allen, Jonathan Winters
and (once more unto the breach) Jerry Lewis. . . . The FCC
orders broadcasters to air anti-smoking commercials.

Super Bowl: It's not an official name, but everybody calls it the Super Bowl, and it becomes television's No. 1 annual sports attraction. Here, in the first Super Bowl game, Jim Taylor of the victorious Green Bay Packers is tackled by Buck Buchanan of the Kansas City Chiefs.

The Smothers Brothers: Their weekly variety show, puckishly titled *The Smothers Comedy Brothers Hour*, debuts in 1967. Its political satire, though mild, makes network executives nervous and will, eventually, lead to the cancellation of the show—in 1969, after a dispute over scripts.

Jerry Lewis: Despite his record of TV failure, Lewis is given another weekly series—and keeps the record intact. Here, while the show lasts, he mugs with comedienne Totie Fields.

252

1967

Carol Burnett: After serving her apprenticeship with Garry Moore, Carol Burnett gets her own weekly hour, and it becomes one of the most popular shows on the air. It is at its best when it satirizes movies — as in this scene, with Burnett spoofing Doris Day, aided by the show's gifted second banana, Harvey Korman.

The Las Vegas Show: This is supposed to be the grand opening of a fourth network—the United Network (known earlier as the Overmyer Network). But this late-night variety show starring Bill Dana (with Abbe Lane here) lasts exactly one month. When it dies, so does the United Network—and its dreams of glory.

253

Mark Twain Tonight: Hal Holbrook's masterful one-man show is brought to TV from the stage for a one-night stand in 1967.

254

Johnny Belinda: Mia Farrow plays the deaf-mute heroine in this made-for-TV movie special.

Africa: On a Sunday in September ABC pre-empts its entire evening schedule and presents a comprehensive four-hour study of Africa and its people — such as this Bushmen maiden.

The Long Childhood of Timmy: A documentary about a brain-damaged boy is a moving experience for viewers. In this scene, 10-year-old Timmy Loughlin gets a boot out of kicking a football.

255

Ironside: Raymond Burr, whose *Perry Mason* series lives on in syndicated re-runs, launches another hit show. This time he's a chief of detectives, Robert Ironside, who is confined to a wheelchair. Other regulars: Don Galloway, Barbara Anderson, Don Mitchell.

Judd for the Defense: This year's descendant of Perry Mason is Clinton Judd, a flamboyant Texas lawyer portrayed by Carl Betz (left, with Stephen Young, playing his junior partner).

256

Mannix: The private eyes are represented in 1967 (and later years) by Joe Mannix (Mike Connors). The first season, Mannix works for a large, computerized agency, but after that he goes freelance.

Custer: In minority-conscious 1967, this attempt to glorify Indian-killer George Armstrong Custer is rejected by most viewers. Wayne Maunder (left) plays Custer.

259

1967

He & She: He is Dick Benjamin and She is Paula Prentiss, and their show becomes a favorite of critics and many viewers—and even the network braintrusters who sheepishly cancel the low-rated series after just one season. The cast includes (l.-r.) Hamilton Camp, Benjamin, Kenneth Mars and Prentiss—plus Jack Cassidy (not pictured).

Cowboy in Africa: Chuck Connors does his riding and roping on a range in Africa, with people like basketball star Bill Russell (right).

Gentle Ben: A friendly bear is the star of a new children's show, along with Clint Howard (pictured) and Dennis Weaver.

The Flying Nun: Preposterous comedy premises are still with us, and so Sister Bertrille (Sally Field) does her good deeds while airborne (her hat has special aerodynamic qualities that enable her to fly).

Captain Nice: Midseason brings two spoofs of Superman—*Mr. Terrific* with Stephen Strimpell; and this one, *Captain Nice*, with Bill Daniels as a timid chemist who accidentally discovers a potion that gives him superhuman powers.

1968
THE YEAR OF CHICAGO

Turmoil, violence, tragedy—1968 is not a year that will be remembered fondly. Martin Luther King and Robert Kennedy are assassinated. The Democrats nominate Hubert Humphrey in Chicago, while police club demonstrators in the streets outside. It is a year of surprises—the Tet offensive, Eugene McCarthy's crusade, Lyndon Johnson's abdication, Mayor Daley's rage, Richard Nixon's comeback. Television is in the thick of it all. . . . And black people are in the thick of television. *Julia* makes Diahann Carroll the first black heroine of a comedy series (unless you want to count *Beulah*). A black family moves into *Peyton Place*. There's a black cowboy in *The Outcasts*. Black faces are finally turning up in commercials. Bill Cosby recounts "Black History: Lost, Stolen or Strayed." Black athletes make militant raised-fist gestures at the Olympics in Mexico City. . . . There are now a full seven movie nights every week. . . . Doing specials for the first time: Ann-Margret, Brigitte Bardot, Petula Clark, Peggy Fleming, James Brown, Wayne Newton, Dick Cavett and Vladimir Horowitz. Princess Lee Radziwill stars in "Laura," Robert Shaw in "Luther," Jack Palance in "Dr. Jekyll and Mr. Hyde," Nicol Williamson and George Segal in "Of Mice and Men." Other acclaimed dramas: "A Case of Libel," "The Thanksgiving Visitor," "The People Next Door." . . . Documentaries: "The Rise and Fall of the Third Reich," "Travels with Charlie," "How Life Begins." . . . Pat Paulsen is running for President, Howard Hughes is trying to take over ABC, and Tiny Tim is trilling. . . . *Laugh-In* is the hit of the year. Other 1968 winners: *60 Minutes, First Tuesday, Here's Lucy* (a revised format for Lucille Ball), *The Doris Day Show, Mayberry RFD, The Mod Squad, Hawaii Five-0, Adam-12, The Name of the Game, The Glen Campbell Goodtime Hour.* Losers: *The Ugliest Girl in Town, The Beautiful Phyllis Diller Show, The Don Rickles Show, The Ghost and Mrs. Muir* and *That's Life.* . . . Commercials are touting longer cigarettes ("A silly millimeter longer"), shaving cream ("Take it off—take it *all* off"), coffee beans ("El Exigente"), air travel ("Is this any way to run an airline?") and cleanliness ("Ring around the collar, ring around the collar" and "Louise Hexter, start wearing cleaner blouses!").

MAYOR RICHARD DALEY
CHICAGO, ILLINOIS

Democratic Convention: TV cameras show scenes of protest and brutality in the streets of Chicago while, inside the hall, Mayor Richard Daley and other party leaders ignore the protests, deny or condone the brutality and don't seem to care that "The whole world is watching" (as chanting demonstrators remind them).

Earthrise: This spectacular view of the rising earth is visible to Apollo 8 astronauts — and TV viewers — during a lunar orbit Dec. 29.

The Undersea World of Jacques Cousteau: Spectacular underwater views are visible too, in the late Sixties and early Seventies, in this series of specials. In this episode, Cousteau's subject is iguanas.

Rowan and Martin's Laugh-In: Most of the jokes are old or silly, but it doesn't matter, because the show moves at a breakneck pace. Its techniques will be copied by many other programs. The first season's cast of "dingalings" includes Judy Carne, Arte Johnson, Ruth Buzzi, Jo Anne Worley, Henry Gibson, Dan Rowan, Dick Martin and (joining up in midseason) Goldie Hawn. Here, Johnson (right) in his "verrry interesting" comic-Nazi routine, is heckled by guest Carl Reiner.

263

Heidi: Jennifer Edwards and Walter Slezak are among the stars of this Alpine drama, but they get a chilly greeting from viewers. Football fans are enraged because NBC has cut off the last few minutes of a thrilling pro game in order to start "Heidi" on schedule. No network will ever dare to cut off a football game again.

1968

Vladimir Horowitz: The piano virtuoso comes to TV in 1968 in a special called "Vladimir Horowitz: A Television Concert at Carnegie Hall."

The People Next Door: The generation gap and the drug problem are dramatized in this special, written by JP Miller and starring (l.-r.) Lloyd Bridges, Deborah Winters and Peter Galman.

The Thanksgiving Visitor: It's a sequel to "A Christmas Memory," as Geraldine Page (with Michael Kearney here) stars in another Truman Capote adaptation.

265

The Doris Day Show: She is one of the first big-name movie stars to try a TV series—and she has better luck than most of the movie people who follow her into TV.

266

Julia: Diahann Carroll stars as a young widow—a nurse—along with Lloyd Nolan, Marc Copage and Betty Beaird.

The Beautiful Phyllis Diller Show: That's the name of Diller's second TV-series attempt, but the result is no more beautiful than it was with the first one (*The Pruitts of Southampton*).

The Ugliest Girl in Town: The town is London and the girl is a boy—Peter Kastner in drag. The the plot has him camping it up as a fashion model because everybody thinks he is a she.

267

The Mod Squad: It's the first of the "relevant" cops-and-robbers shows. Peggy Lipton, Michael Cole and Clarence Williams III (l.-r.) play an undercover police trio specializing in the crimes and problems of misguided youth.

The Outcasts: After the Civil War a white Southerner (Don Murray) and an ex-slave (Otis Young) form an uneasy partnership and ride west.

Hawaii Five-0: The cops in this series operate in Hawaii. Jack Lord stars as the head of a special unit of the Hawaii state police. In this episode he appears with Simon Oakland (left) and Toru Shimada (right).

The Prisoner: The most unorthodox —and provoca- tive—series of 1968 is this Brit- ish import about a man (Patrick McGoohan) who wakes up in a strange town in which inexplica- ble things happen and from which there is no es- cape.

269

1969
THE YEAR OF THE MOON MEN

It is as incredible a sight as the world has ever seen—a man is walking on the moon! And millions of people the world over are watching him do it—fuzzily but still visibly—on television. . . . Meanwhile, back on earth, President Nixon is in the White House, Vice President Agnew is accusing the networks of bias and Sen. Edward Kennedy is on TV explaining what happened at Chappaquiddick. It is the year of My Lai, the Chicago Eight, the death of Dwight D. Eisenhower. A timely documentary asks "Who Killed Lake Erie?" . . . And many disenchanted viewers ask who killed the Smothers Brothers, when CBS cancels the Brothers' irreverent series after a long wrangle. . . . Doctor shows are back (*Marcus Welby, M.D., Medical Center*). Variety series are in vogue (Tom Jones, Johnny Cash, Leslie Uggams, Jim Nabors and—again—Andy Williams). So are talk shows (Dick Cavett, David Frost, Merv Griffin). . . . *Sesame Street* and *The Forsyte Saga* demonstrate that the Public Broadcasting Service has definitely arrived. . . . Specials showcase Jose Feliciano, Engelbert Humperdinck, Rod McKuen, Mama Cass Elliot, Dionne Warwicke, Simon and Garfunkel, The Supremes, Burt Bacharach, Woody Allen, Arthur Rubinstein, two Frank Sinatras—Sr. and Jr.—and a lad named Flip Wilson. . . . Dramas are sparse in 1969. They include "Teacher, Teacher" and the Royal Shakespeare Company's "A Midsummer Night's Dream." . . . Joe Namath and the New York Jets upset the Baltimore Colts in the Super Bowl, 16-7. And the Amazin' Mets defeat the Baltimore Orioles in the World Series. . . . *Peyton Place* and *The Late Show* end long runs. *Turn On* ends a short one—it is a one-episode debacle. . . . ABC introduces a made-for-TV movie series (*The Movie of the Week*). Hugh Hefner returns to TV with *Playboy After Dark*. *Hee Haw* is born, and *My World . . . and Welcome to It, The Bold Ones, The Courtship of Eddie's Father, The Brady Bunch, Room 222, Love, American Style, The Survivors* (nighttime soap opera, Harold Robbins style), . . . *Then Came Bronson* and an item titled *Jimmy Durante Presents the Lennon Sisters Hour*. . . . Commercials proclaim, "You've come a long way, baby" and "You in a heap o' trouble, boy."

Moon Walk: The picture is dim and blurry, but there it is, for all the world to see—Neil Armstrong moving out of his spaceship, slowly descending a ladder and setting foot on the moon. And much of the world *does* see it, as the historic achievement is beamed to TV sets all over the globe, by satellite.

Sesame Street: PBS's biggest hit is aimed at preschool children, but it also entrances many of their parents. A large part of the show's appeal can be attributed to Jim Henson's Muppets, including these two—Ernie (left) and Sherlock Hemlock.

Black Journal: It's one of the first of many series aimed at black viewers in the late Sixties. In this episode Imamu Amiri Baraka (LeRoi Jones) is the speaker.

The Forsyte Saga: Kenneth More (left) and Eric Porter lead a huge cast in the serialized version of Galsworthy's novels, borrowed from the BBC.

1969

Dick Cavett: His show gains favor with viewers who are not satisfied with the level of discourse on other talk shows. But there are not enough of them to suit ABC, and in 1972 the network will decide to cut Cavett back to one week per month. Here, he greets Anthony Quinn (left).

David Frost: His show arrives around the same time as Cavett's and appeals to a similar audience. But it is a syndicated series—no network—and it is heading for a 1972 axe too. Frost's guest here is Rose Kennedy.

Merv Griffin: CBS chooses him to carry its standard into the late-night ratings battle. But the show never jells, and Griffin also will leave network TV in 1972. His sidekick (left) is Arthur Treacher.

275

Leslie Uggams: A *Sing Along with Mitch* alumna, she fails too—in the time slot from which the Smothers Brothers have been evicted.

Tom Jones: The new darling of the menopause set, he gets his own show in 1969 too.

1969

Johnny Cash: 1969 is a good year for country music— good enough to give Johnny Cash his own weekly series, from Nashville.

Jim Nabors: He graduates from *Gomer Pyle* to a variety series, but it's too big a jump, and the show fails.

277

Hee Haw: It seems to be an incompatible combination—the technical zip of *Laugh-In* applied to barnyard humor—but it adds up to strong ratings. Three of the regulars are (l.-r.) Gunilla Hutton, Junior Samples and Dianna Scott.

My World . . . and Welcome to It: Based tenuously on James Thurber's writings, and using his cartoons, this series stars William Windom (playing chess with Lisa Gerritsen).

1969

The Courtship of Eddie's Father: The warm relationship between father (Bill Bixby) and son (Brandon Cruz) gives this family sitcom a special flavor. Other cast members are Miyoshi Umeki and Jimmie Komack.

Love, American Style: Each week's show contains several episodes performed by guest stars, plus blackouts featuring a troupe of regulars. This playlet casts Tiny Tim as a vampire with Judy Carne and Robert Reed.

1969

Marcus Welby, M.D.: The doctor show comes back strong in 1969, as this story of a general practitioner is the most popular new series of the year. Robert Young is Welby, James Brolin his youthful partner, and Elena Verdugo their nurse. Here, Welby treats an Indian from a reservation (Peter Duel).

Room 222: Lloyd Haynes and Karen Valentine (pictured) star with Denise Nicholas and Michael Constantine in this comedy-drama series, set in a Los Angeles high school.

. . . Then Came Bronson: Laconic Jim Bronson (Michael Parks) goes varooming around the country searching for the meaning of life, in this low-key drama series.

The Survivors: They don't survive long, despite a high-powered author-creator (Harold Robbins) and cast (Lana Turner and Kevin McCarthy—pictured—and George Hamilton and Ralph Bellamy).

281

1969

Joe Namath: He leads the New York Jets to an upset win over the Baltimore Colts, as the AFL finally achieves parity with the NFL—and Namath achieves a unique kind of stardom that goes beyond the football field.

Teacher, Teacher: The story of a mentally retarded boy (Billy Schulman) and his tutor (David McCallum) becomes a moving TV drama. Ossie Davis and George Grizzard are also in the cast.

Woody Allen: The comedian-writer-director tries a TV special in 1969, with Candice Bergen as one of his guests.

Chappaquiddick: Sen. Edward Kennedy uses television in 1969 to attempt to explain what happened when a car he was driving went off a bridge, drowning his passenger, Mary Jo Kopechne, and changing his political prospects.

1970
THE YEAR OF RELEVANCE

"Relevance" is what network strategists think people want, and they pile it on, in one socially conscious series after another—*The Young Lawyers, Storefront Lawyers, The Senator, Matt Lincoln, Headmaster* and an all-black rendition of *Barefoot in the Park*. It turns out, however, that most viewers still are blissfully seeking irrelevance, and all these well-meaning ventures fail. . . . *The Flip Wilson Show* is hot. *Mary Tyler Moore, The Partridge Family* and *The Odd Couple* are warm enough to survive. *Nancy, The Immortal, Dan August*, Don Knotts and Tim Conway shows, and Danny Thomas's *Make Room for Granddaddy* are out cold. . . . 1970 is the year of Cambodia, Kent State, hard hats, Earth Day and women's lib; but for TV's news departments, it's the year of Tricia Nixon's White House tour, a glimpse of Britain's Royal Family, and "The World of the Beaver." The most potent documentaries come from PBS—Frederick Wiseman's "Hospital" and a four-part account of the trial of a Black Panther. . . . *Civilisation* comes to PBS from BBC, as the public network launches its first season as a nationwide network (five nights a week). . . . Chet Huntley retires, Harry Reasoner jumps from CBS to ABC, Apollo 13 turns back after malfunctioning on the way to the moon, Tom Dempsey boots a 63-yard field goal, CBS boots Red Skelton, cigarette commercials are snuffed out, Monday-night football begins, and Edmund Muskie seems to be a shoo-in for the 1972 Democratic Presidential nomination after an effective Election Eve TV address. . . . Dramas: "The Andersonville Trial," "Hamlet" (Richard Chamberlain), "Marat/Sade," "David Copperfield," "A Storm in Summer" and a highly praised tailored-for-TV-movie, "My Sweet Charlie." . . . Entertainment specials: "Annie, the Women in the Life of a Man," "Harry and Lena," "George M!" and showcases for Raquel Welch, and Smokey Robinson and the Miracles. . . . 95.2 percent of Americans now have television—39.3 percent in color. . . . A heart-shaped dumpling is one ingredient of 1970's favorite commercial. Other commercials say, "Mama mia, that's-a some-a spicy meat-a-ball" and "I haven't lost a daughter, I've gained a dandruff shampoo" and "My girdle is killing me."

Lawyer and Senator: Typical of TV's "relevance" kick are these two series. *The Young Lawyers* (top) is about a group of attorneys practicing public-service law in Boston. Zalman King (with client Flora Plumb here) stars as Aaron Silverman, with Lee J. Cobb and Judy Pace. *The Senator* (below) becomes part of *The Bold Ones*, wins critical applause, but lasts only one season, although the doctor and lawyer shows it alternates with are both renewed. Hal Holbrook (right) portrays Sen. Hays Stowe, with Michael Tolan as his aide.

Royal Family: This documentary gives viewers an unusually intimate glimpse of Britain's queen and her family —including the two princes, Charles (left) and Andrew.

Civilisation: PBS's big series in 1970 is another British import— *Civilisation*, with Lord Clark of Saltwood (Kenneth Clark) delivering erudite and beautifully illustrated lectures on the development of Western culture.

286

The Journey of Robert F. Kennedy: It is an *ABC Movie of the Week* episode, the only documentary amid an assortment of melodramas. This family portrait was taken at the Kennedys' Hickory Hill estate.

Tricia Nixon: She guides a tour of the family living quarters at the White House, as part of the *60 Minutes* series, with Harry Reasoner and Mike Wallace.

Flip Wilson: His show clicks with all segments of the viewing audience. Here, he signs off in his customary fashion with Tony Randall, as Lena Horne looks on.

Monday Night Football: Pro football's bold move into prime time makes Howard Cosell a national (and controversial) celebrity and is a success with everybody except the exasperated wives of bleary-eyed football fanatics. Here, Sonny Jurgenson calls signals for the Washington Redskins.

Annie, the Women in the Life of a Man: Anne Bancroft displays her versatility in sketches with various men, including Robert Merrill (pictured).

George M!: It's an abbreviated version of the Broadway musical about George M. Cohan, with (l.-r.) Bernadette Peters, Jack Cassidy, Anita Gillette, Joel Grey and Nanette Fabray.

Here's Lucy: Lucille Ball opens her season with Elizabeth Taylor and Richard Burton as guest stars. The plot has something to do with Liz's $1,500,000 diamond ring, which gets stuck on Lucy's finger.

The Odd Couple: Jack Klugman and Tony Randall work smoothly together in the TV series based on Neil Simon's play and movie.

The Partridge Family: They're a pop singing group who travel around the country in an old school bus. The family includes (l.-r.) Susan Dey, Shirley Jones, Suzanne Crough, David Cassidy and Danny Bonaduce.

Mary Tyler Moore: This new series displays sharp comedy writing and a gifted acting ensemble, including Mary Tyler Moore and Ted Knight (pictured), plus Valerie Harper, Ed Asner, Cloris Leachman and Gavin McLeod.

David Copperfield: An all-star cast, including Sir Laurence Olivier and Richard Attenborough (pictured), appear in this adaptation of Dickens' novel.

Hamlet: Richard Chamberlain, who became a Shakespearian actor after *Dr. Kildare* folded, returns to TV for a night as Hamlet.

292

The Andersonville Trial: It is the first of several dramatic triumphs for *Hollywood Television Theatre*, on public television. William Shatner (left) and Richard Basehart star.

A Storm in Summer: Peter Ustinov is the owner of a smalltown delicatessen who plays host to a boy from Harlem in this play by Rod Serling.

293

1971
THE YEAR OF THE BIGOT

Astounding. A situation comedy about a bigot not only gets on the air but become's America's favorite television series. *All in the Family* scores an extraordinary victory over the networks' traditional aversion to controversy in their entertainment programs, and the viewers' presumed preference for blandness in theirs. . . . Big-name, high-priced movie stars fare poorly in their TV series—James Stewart, Anthony Quinn, Tony Curtis, Shirley MacLaine, Glenn Ford all go down the drain. So do some former TV whiz kids attempting to repeat earlier successes—James Garner, David Janssen, Don Adams. Bobby Sherman's show doesn't make it. Sonny and Cher's does. Sandy Duncan's *Funny Face* and Peter Falk's *Columbo* are hits. Pearl Bailey, *Longstreet, Sarge, The Chicago Teddy Bears* aren't. *Cannon, The New Dick Van Dyke Show* and *Owen Marshall: Counselor at Law* do okay. . . . During a year of confrontation and conflict in the United States—the Pentagon Papers, the Laos incursion, the Calley trial, the largest peace demonstration in history—the networks are presenting documentaries on Scotland Yard, auto racing, endangered wildlife and expectant motherhood. . . . "The Selling of the Pentagon" is a lonely reminder that investigative reporting is not completely dead on commercial TV. . . . PBS's lineup adds *The Great American Dream Machine, The Electric Company, Masterpiece Theatre's* "The First Churchills" and William F. Buckley's *Firing Line*. And some powerful drama specials: "Hogan's Goat," "U.S.A.," "Paradise Lost," "A Memory of Two Mondays," "Home" (with Gielgud and Richardson). . . . Dramas on the other networks: "The Six Wives of Henry VIII," "The Homecoming," "All the Way Home," "Jane Eyre," "The Price," "The Snow Goose" and the most successful made-for-TV movie yet—"Brian's Song." . . . Other specials: "Julie and Carol at Lincoln Center," "Dames at Sea," and shows starring Diahann Carroll, Goldie Hawn, Arte Johnson, Jascha Heifetz and George Plimpton. . . . A new FCC rule compels the networks to relinquish a half hour of nightly prime time. . . . Merv Griffin decides to abandon CBS's late-night show, John Chancellor becomes NBC's anchor man, Frank McGee replaces Hugh Downs on *Today*. And, after 23 years, *The Ed Sullivan Show* is no more.

All in the Family: Carroll O'Connor as Archie Bunker, and Jean Stapleton as his "dingbat" wife Edith are the stars of this trend-setting comedy series. It deals with topics—political, ethnic and sexual—that till now have been taboo in American entertainment programs. Rob Reiner and Sally Struthers play the young members of the quarrelsome household.

President Nixon: The country's No. 1 football fan turns up often on televised sports events. Here, he talks with Frank Gifford (right) at a Hall of Fame football game in Canton, Ohio, as Roone Arledge (left), head of ABC Sports, listens.

Vice President Agnew: Though critical of its news coverage, Spiro Agnew is quite at home on TV. Here, he and his wife and granddaughter appear with Dinah Shore (right) on *Dinah's Place.*

296

1971

Johnny Mann: His *Stand Up and Cheer* starts as a patriotic special, then becomes a syndicated series.

John Wayne: In the early 1970's the veteran movie actor appears frequently in TV, often in shows extolling the glories of America. This one, in 1971, is "The American West of John Ford."

William F. Buckley: His *Firing Line* debate series, which started in syndication, moves into a weekly PBS berth in 1971.

297

The Six Wives of Henry VIII: CBS imports this series of six historical dramas from Britain for summer viewing in 1971. Keith Michell plays Henry.

Brian's Song: Billy Dee Williams (left) and James Caan are the leads in this movie recounting the deep friendship of football players Gale Sayers and Brian Piccolo, and Piccolo's fatal illness.

1971

The Snow Goose: It's the touching story (by Paul Gallico) of a girl (Jenny Agutter—pictured), a recluse (Richard Harris) and the bird they nurse back to health, during World War II.

The Price: Arthur Miller's play is adapted for television, with George C. Scott and Colleen Dewhurst (pictured) and Barry Sullivan and David Burns in the cast.

Home: Superlative acting by Sir John Gielgud (left) and Sir Ralph Richardson enrich this disturbing play.

299

Columbo: Peter Falk's performance as a rumpled police detective makes this every-three-weeks series one of the few popular new shows of the year.

The Man and the City: Drama series with politicians as heroes have never been very successful in TV, and this one is no exception, despite the presence of Anthony Quinn as Mayor Tom Alcala.

1971

Longstreet: He's a blind insurance investigator, played by James Franciscus.

Sarge: George Kennedy is a priest who used to be a cop.

301

Tony Awards: The most entertaining of all televised awards shows is this Tony program in 1971. It reprises great moments from Broadway musicals, including this scene from "Fiddler on the Roof," with Zero Mostel.

The Great American Dream Machine: A highly imaginative magazine-format show makes its appearance on PBS in 1971. Its only regular cast member is rotund Marshall Efron, who delivers satirical commentaries on consumer products.

Sonny & Cher: Their variety series scores well enough during a summer tryout in 1971 to give Sonny and Cher Bono a regular-season slot the following winter.

Pure Goldie: *Laugh-In* alumna Goldie Hawn is given a special of her own. Here, she does a skit with Bob Dishy.

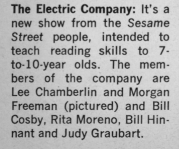

The Electric Company: It's a new show from the *Sesame Street* people, intended to teach reading skills to 7-to-10-year olds. The members of the company are Lee Chamberlin and Morgan Freeman (pictured) and Bill Cosby, Rita Moreno, Bill Hinnant and Judy Graubart.

303

1972
THE YEAR OF POLITICS--OLD AND NEW

Politics dominates television in 1972, as Democrat George McGovern attempts to evict the White House's Republican tenant, Richard Nixon, in what is billed as a battle between the "new politics" and the old. . . . Before Election Day arrives, however, TV newscasts are filled with other extraordinary events—Nixon's trips to China and the Soviet Union; bombing, blockading and negotiating in Vietnam; the shooting of George Wallace; the brief Vice-Presidential candidacy of Tom Eagleton; the final chapters in the Apollo program. . . . Politics plays a role in entertainment programs too, as CBS revives "Of Thee I Sing" and PBS suppresses a Woody Allen special containing political jibes. . . . The drama department carries some big imports—"Elizabeth R," "The Search for the Nile," "The Life of Leonardo da Vinci" and the Russian movie version of "War and Peace." Home-grown plays include Odets's "Awake and Sing," Lorraine Hansberry's "To Be Young, Gifted and Black," Kurt Vonnegut's "Between Time and Timbuctoo," Loring Mandel's "Particular Men" and a hard-hitting movie, "The Glass House." *Hallmark Hall of Fame* racks up its 100th TV production, "The Hands of Cormac Joyce." . . . Most impressive of the new network series is Alistair Cooke's *America*. Other series are vehicles for stars (Julie Andrews, Bill Cosby); adaptations (*Anna and the King, M*A*S*H*); and the usual mixture of comedy (*Maude, Bridget Loves Bernie, The Little People, The Bob Newhart Show*), action (*Banacek, Hec Ramsey, Search, The Men, The Rookies, The Streets of San Francisco*) and fiasco (*Me and the Chimp*). . . . The nation settles back to watch the most exhaustive and expert Olympics coverage ever—and is suddenly plunged into a heart-sickening day of terror and murder in Munich, as 11 Israeli athletes and officials are killed by cold-blooded Arab zealots. . . . The World Series schedules more night games to sell more cars and razor blades to more viewers. . . . The death of Dan Blocker upsets *Bonanza*'s equilibrium. . . . ABC gives up on Dick Cavett, announcing that his show will be cut back to one week per month. . . . And, as The Television Years continue to roll on, with a momentum all their own, their latest contributions to the American vernacular are "Try it, you'll like it" and "I can't believe I ate the whole thing."

Nixon vs. McGovern: It is a bitterly fought campaign between President Nixon (top, with his wife), whose trips to China and Russia give his re-election chances a boost; and Senator McGovern, who confounds pundits and pollsters by capturing the nomination but still is buried under a Nixon landslide on Election Day.

Education: Fundamental questions about the quality and techniques and goals of education are being asked in 1972 —and examined in such TV specials as "What Did You Learn in School Today?"

Busing: This highly emotional issue is the subject of several TV documentaries. In this one, "Busing: Some Voices from the South," a black social worker and a Ku Klux Klan leader warily exchange views in Durham, N.C.

Labor: The working man's place in American society—and his attitudes—seem to be undergoing a change in 1972. It is a story that turns up on TV frequently now. This is Edward Wojciechowski, an automobile worker who is seen in a documentary called "The Blue Collar Workers."

307

Elizabeth R: A bravura performance by Glenda Jackson holds this mini-series together. This is her death scene, in the final episode.

308

That Certain Summer: TV drama breaks new ground in this *ABC Movie of the Week* about a homosexual (Hal Holbrook) and his son (Scott Jacoby).

The Search for the Nile: Michael Gough plays Dr. Livingstone in this historical-drama mini-series.

The Glass House: Life inside a prison is realistically depicted in a Truman Capote-inspired movie. Vic Morrow (right) performs with real inmates of Utah State Prison.

The Woman I Love: Richard Chamberlain impersonates Edward VIII in this dramatization of his love affair and abdication.

309

Liza Minnelli: Her special, "Liza with a Z," helps get the 1972-73 TV season off to a fast start.

Banyon: The hardboiled private eye of the Thirties returns in the person of Miles Banyon (Robert Forster).

310

1972

Maude: Liberal pretensions are punctured in this spin-off from *All in the Family*, starring Beatrice Arthur with William Macy.

Kung Fu: The most offbeat action entry of 1972 is a monthly series that finds David Carradine playing Caine, a Chinese-American mystic who wanders through the Old West.

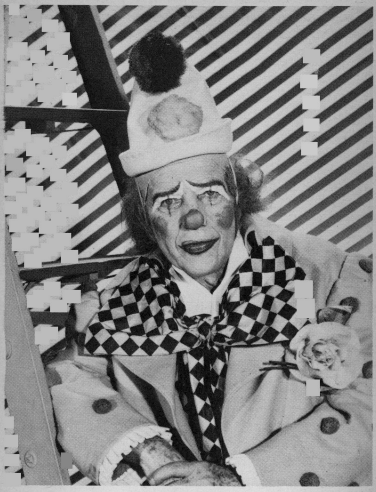

Clown: In 1972, Ed Sullivan, no longer welcome in weekly television, is producing and appearing in occasional specials. This one is called "Clownaround."

INDEX OF HIGHLIGHTS